Praise for The Big Dog Diaries

"I read this book quite by accident. A friend gave it to me and while I was eating lunch one day, I casually read the first few pages and was hooked by this big ugly dog's story. Anyone who is a dog lover will fall in love with Big." - Andrew C. Palmer

"A very quick (too quick!) read. I love Laz's style. If you are looking for one of those annoyingly cloying books about a cutesy dog, try something else. If you want gritty realism, try something else. If you want a delightfully droll read, then settle in for a very pleasant time. I'm going to make this my go-to book when gifting people who like animals." - Mary L. Herrick

"I had a hard time putting [the book] down. Written in a unique style, this is a book that dog people, runners, walkers, and everybody else with a heart will enjoy." - Harald Vaessin "HEFV"

"A story about a pit bull dog may be offputting to some; but one must forget all the negative things associated with this breed in this case. Lazarus Lake is a great storyteller. His prose style is different from probably anything you have read before; but it flows smoothly and keeps the reader interested. Whether big is as special as he seems because of his genetics, or the training he received from laz, or a combination of the two is not important to the quality of the stories. He provides entertainment for his human family; and these stories shall provide great entertainment for all those fortunate enough to read them." - Dan Baglione

the big dog diaries

part 1: my name is big
part 2: big adventures
part 3: big tails
part 4: the big year (summer and fall)
part 5: the big year (winter and spring)

the big dog diaries
part 5: the big year
(winter and spring)

Lazarus Lake

The information in this book is meant to entertain and not to replace proper training advice. All forms of exercise contain inherent risks that the reader should be aware of before starting any sort of exercise program. The publisher recommends that you follow any directions given to you by your doctor before modifying your current exercise program. Mention of specific companies, products, organizations or authorities does not imply endorsement on the part of the author or publisher, or does it imply that those entities in any way endorse the author, publisher or this book. All internet addresses in this book were accurate as of the time this book went to print.

This book is Copyright © 2013 by Gary Cantrell (the "Author"). All Rights Reserved. Published in the United States of America. No part of this book may be reproduced or transmitted in any form or by any means, electronic or mechanical, including photocopying, recording, or by an information storage and retrieval system, except by a reviewer who may quote brief passages in a review to be printed in a magazine, newspaper, blog, or website, without permission in writing from the Author. For information, please contact the Author by mail at the address below.

bigdogdiaries.com
drystoneman@hotmail.com

First Printed Edition, September 2014

Printed in the United States of America
Print ISBN-10: 1500165549
Print ISBN-13: 978-1500165543
BISAC: Pets / Dogs / Breeds

Published by Trail Trotter Press / Run to Win, LLC (the "Publisher").

Trail Trotter Press
824 Roosevelt Trail #203
Windham, ME, 04062
www.TrailTrotterPress.com

Table of Contents

FOREWARD 1
WINTER 2013 3
    01-01-13 THE PORCH DOG 5
    01-03-13 DOGS INVENTED SOCIAL MEDIA 9
    01-04-13 THE COYOTE HUNTERS 13
    01-06-13 THE BIG QUESTION 17
    01-07-13 HARBINGERS OF SPRING 19
    01-14-13 EVERY DOG HAS HIS DAY 23
    01-25-13 THE BIG GOOBER 29
    01-28-13 BIG PROVIDENCE 31
    01-31-13 BIG DECISIONS 35
    02-02-13 THE BIG SNOW 41
    02-05-13 REQUIEM FOR THE TRAILER DOGS 49
    02-10-13 TRAILER DOGS, THE FINAL STORY 53
    02-11-13 THE WHITE TRAILER DOG MAKES A BREAK FOR IT ... 57
    02-12-13 THE BIG CATASTROPHE 59
    02-18-13 PUPPY LOVE 65
    02-23-13 TERROR IN BIGISTAN 71
    02-24-13 CROWMUNICATION 75
    02-28-13 THE PURPLE DRESS 81
    03-05-13 COYOTE HUNTERS DON'T HELP 87
    03-09-13 THE TALKING DOG 89
    03-12-13 THE SENSITIVE GUY 91
    03-17-13 A BIG FUTURE 97
    03-23-13 THE BIG STINK 101
    03-24-13 SWEETIE 105
    04-02-13 THE BIG ORGANIZATIONAL CHART 109
    04-07-13 BIG GREETINGS 115

SPRING 2013 117
- 04-08-13 THE BIG INCIDENT 119
- 04-15-13 THE BIG COMPETITION 125
- 04-17-13 BIG BIRDS 129
- 04-19-13 BIG ON DUTY 133
- 04-25-13 A BIG'S WORK IS NEVER DONE 137
- 04-26-13 THE BIG FURBALL 141
- 05-08-13 THE BIG VET VISIT 145
- 05-10-13 THE BIG LAUGH 152
- 05-12-13 REALLY? 155
- 05-14-13 HEY-HEY, BOO-BOO 159
- 05-15-13 THE BIG SHAPE-SHIFTER (PART 1) 161
- 05-15-13 VEGAS KNOWS THEIR STUFF 167
- 05-17-13 THE BIG SHAPE-SHIFTER (PART 2) 169
- 05-26-13 BIG THE BALONEY HOUND 173
- 05-26-13 BIG REHAB 175
- 06-07-13 BIG BETA SITE 179
- 06-10-13 BABY FOOD A-LA-DIABLA (PART 1) 183
- 06-10-13 BABY FOOD A-LA-DIABLA (PART 2) 189
- 06-10-13 BABY FOOD A-LA-DIABLA (PART 3) 193
- 06-14-13 THE BIG WINNER 195

ABOUT THE AUTHOR 201

Foreward

Some might consider it divine providence that brought the Big Dog into my life. Arriving at the time he did, Big was there at just the right moments to accompany me through major transitions.

A lifelong long distance runner, I had just incurred the injury which would end that running career, and leave me with only the option to walk. At the time Big arrived, I still thought I would work my way through this problem, the same way I always had before. Big was there, with his quiet acceptance of the hand he had been dealt, along with his refusal to be less than joyous in the playing of those cards. With Big at my side, I walked into a new chapter in my life; discovering that the love of covering long distances on foot did not have to end, just because I could no longer run them.

A career accountant; at the same time as my relationship with the Big was transitioning into a partnership, I found myself involuntarily retired. While I thought I was at the peak of my career; with decades of experience to draw on, yet still vital enough that the accumulating effects of time had not begun to impact my abilities, the world had decided that I was too old to begin anew. It would have been easy to grow bitter at the perceived rejection, and wallow in self-pity at having become a member of the discarded generation. I had only to look at the Big; gentle, affectionate, and passionate in his love of people, yet treated with horror and revulsion because of the reputation of his breed, to find that option impossible. Big bore his burden with quiet dignity, I felt obligated to live up to that example. As "me and big" walked our daily patrols around the "big territory" I came to realize that we had both found ourselves a place in the world. Surrounded by the beauty of peaceful farms and woodlands, and accepted for who we are by our neighbors and friends, we really had everything we needed.

It brings a secret smile when I read the description of the Big Dog Diaries, and it refers to Big as a "rescue dog." I never rescued the Big. He showed up at my home, just when he was needed the most, and decided that he belonged to me. How he came to choose me, I will never know for sure... Big keeps his secrets well. Perhaps it really was divine providence.

My Name is Big recounts the arrival of the Big, and how he went from a tolerated presence, for whom we only wanted to find a permanent home, to a member of the family. Big Adventures and Big Tails tell the story of our journey from a mere man and his dog, to a partnership.

A partnership like ours is almost like a marriage. As "me and big" greet each day of our travel through life, there are always new adventures just around the next bend, or over the next hill. With his remarkable intelligence, and his desire to please his master, my big friend always has new surprises for me. The Big Year is just that. It is the accumulated stories of one unique year in "big territory." It begins in June, immediately following the race which concluded Big Tails. The race in which, thanks to my training under "coach big," I once again got to savor the taste of pushing myself to the limit, despite my bad leg. From there the Big Year follows us through the seasons of Summer, Fall, Winter, and Spring and back to my, now annual, June race. As usual, there is no real plot; just the daily adventures that are life with Big.

Me and big hope you enjoy our stories!

winter 2013

hello.
my name is big,
and i love the winter.

i love to feel the cold wind in my face
when master takes me walking.
the cold air makes me want to run and play.
i feel like a puppy again.

we walk on the trails a lot in the winter
and i can walk with no leash.
i run up the trail as fast as i can go.
then i run back to master.
i jump over rocks and logs.
i love to play in the woods.

sometimes in the winter
master takes me for walks in the snow..
when i run in the snow

it flies in the air all around me.

when there is no snow,
i can play in the deep leaves.

in the winter it feels good to sleep in the sun.
in the winter it feels good to snuggle in my warm bed.

winter is the perfect time of year.

i love the winter.

i wish it lasted all year.

big

01-01-13
the porch dog

after the last tarp was destroyed on christmas eve
i was in kind of a bind.
well, actually big was in kind of a bind.

there was no dry place for him to stay out on his cable.
going to murfreesboro to try to find a real canvas tarp
was out of the question.
no sane person goes to town on christmas eve.

so i rounded up a couple of used dog pillow beds,
and an old sleeping bag.
putting them back in the corner behind the porch fireplace
i made big a nice bed.

big approved of his new digs,
settling in without a complaint.
i left him with the admonition to "stay on the porch."

big followed his instructions admirably.
too admirably.
that afternoon i went out on the porch,
and big went straight to the top of the steps
and looked at me; pleading.
being a little bit slow,
i thought maybe he wanted to go back to the bigloo.
but, as soon as we left the porch, the poor big fella raced to the woods....

and peed for about 5 minutes.
if he was supposed to "stay on the porch"
then he was going to "stay on the porch."

over the two days we worked out a routine.
big left the porch when me & him went walking.
he left the porch to "go" in the woods.
and he left the porch to greet visitors,
after which he returned to his new big-place.

the 26th rolled around,
and i just took him to practice with me.
i thought after the first time big went to practice,
that he would not want to go wait in the car again.
i underestimated the big.
sitting in the car for two and a half or three hours,
and watching the gymn door for me to come back out...

he thinks that is a good big job.

the next three days were a different story.
our distant christmas tournament meant leaving in the early
afternoon, and returning late at night.
big could not go.

i fashioned the best shelter i could out of the remains of his tarp,
and put him on his cable.
he went in the bigloo and lay down.
i figured he would be fine until i got home.
and amy would be home in a couple of hours,
just in case.

when amy got home,
a collarless big was sleeping on the back porch.

and thus it went all three days.
put big on his cable,
big goes in the bigloo and settles down.
five minutes after i leave,
big is sleeping on the back porch, collarless.

i tried removing his bed.
a little later i looked out to see a shivering big,
lying on the cold bare stone, and looking forlorn.

i put his bed back.

i miss the day when i thought i was smarter than any dog...
or at least was smart enough to contain them.
crates, pens, chains, and cables...

big will not be contained.
he will stay on the porch on command.
but will not stay anywhere by physical restraint.

the big year: winter and spring

i have to admit,
i feel a lot better with him on the porch with it raining every day.
he has a nice dry place to be.
sophie collected all his bones one by one during her own bathroom trips
and brought them up to the porch....
dropping them when she saw big.
little has shown no real inclination to steal them again...
big is not on a cable!

big naps, and plays with his bones.
(carefully, so he doesn't throw them off the porch!)
he sits in my chair when the sun is on it.
he waits anxiously for me to come take him for his walk...during several of which we have ended up getting soaked in the rain.
he looks in the doors or windows and wags his tail to see us.
and he goes to greet visitors...

the greeting visitors being the part that worries me.
not everyone sees that huge head and gaping mouth;
that thick neck and powerful shoulders;
and sees a sweet natured, affectionate puppy.

i am just not certain what is my next move.
big has decided that he is a porch dog.

laz

01-03-13
dogs invented social media

you heard me right
(or maybe read me right)
dogs invented social media.
the more time passes, with me spending more time with dogs than people, the more i have become aware of their complicated and intense social world.

as big and i patrol our territory each day,
i have come to recognize the pattern of his pee-mails and poopbook posts.
he doesn't just randomly pee every hundred feet.
every pee-mail has a specific placement,
and is intended for a specific audience.

he leaves messages in front of the homes of every dog on our routes, even dogs that i didn't realize existed for years.
he leaves pee-mails where game trails cross the roads.
some of the trails i can even see with my inferior human senses, restricted, basically, to vision.
others i eventually recognized because big is always engaged there; sniffing around intently and finally leaving his pee-mails.
there are a couple of sites where his hackles raise as he snuffles about.
whatever crosses there, it is something big does not like at all.
some of the crossings i figured out because i kept seeing deer there, or turkeys, or some other animal.
others only big knows what member of his social world crosses.

poopbook took me longer to figure out.
at first i just thought big was just relieving himself.
i mistook deliberate messages for simple bodily functions.
the fact that he consistently hit the same spots,
i attributed to it just taking him that long to work up the need to go.

i did think it odd that he went to such pains to poop on prominent high spots;
"wouldn't it be easier to poop in a low spot, big fella?"

the big dog diaries

i found it curious that after pooping,
he would often top off his effort with a squirt of clear liquid.
i wondered how his digestive tract managed that little trick.

but, as me and big take our daily hikes, there is a lot of time to observe and reflect.
eventually i came to recognize that big's mental map of our territory is very different than mine.
i only have the roads and trails that are used by humans.
big's map has many thoroughfares which have no human traffic.
and on the big map, his poop sites just happen to correspond to major junctions.
what seemed like random locations are hardly the dead zones that my initial human judgement deemed them.

and the little shot of clear liquid...
from back in the recesses of my brain i remembered that dogs (like many animals) have anal glands.
and i remembered hearing that bigs have hyperdeveloped adrenal glands.
that had only sounded like another pit bull legend,
until i noted that big does indeed behave as if he has supercharged adrenal glands.
i had never seen any other dog squirt clear liquid like big,
but perhaps all of the big's glands are supersized.

and so, while i have been training the big, he has had his own lessons to teach me.
i have come to recognize that the random piles of poop that he is so interested in the first time he sees them
are not so random at all.
and the animals around us,
with their senses of smell able to pick up subtleties that we struggle to convey in written language,
are peeing, pooping, and rubbing against stuff to leave messages which make our own social media seem like crude grunts and gestures.

now that i understand who is training who,
i am proud that i am learning my lessons so well.
the other day we came on a new dog over in millersburg.
me & big deemed him the christmas dog,

the big year: winter and spring

because he turned up a few days after christmas, and was wearing a shiny new red collar.
there had been a dog at that house all along,
a black and white border collie that always kept a safe distance and just watched us pass.

that morning, as we walked past, i saw big suddenly turn his head and stare intently.
i turned my head to see what he was looking at,
just as i picked up the sound of the dog's charging feet.
it was some sort of terrier,
short greyhound-grey fur (very clean and neat looking) with a shiny red collar.
altho only about a 20 or 25 pound dog,
it looked lean and long-legged....

of course, if you hang around with big,
almost any dog looks lean and long-legged.
big's position next to me clearly told me the dog was not coming in a friendly manner,
which meshed with how he looked to me.
so i took a step towards him, raised my trainer to point it at him, and said;
"you better think twice."
the dog, which had not made a sound (outside the thundering of his feet)
executed a neat curl cut, and returned the way it had come,
never dropping below top speed.
he did not look back.

i saw the border collie had come off the porch
(for the first time ever)
to see what was going to happen.
seeing the other dog turn tail,
he was satisfied that we were as scary as he'd always imagined and turned to beat a path back to the porch.

as me and big turned to continue walking,
i saw a man come bursting out the door of the house.
i raised my trainer to wave at him and kept going.
he stopped and stared at us, moving only to let his new dog run

in the door.
he did not return my wave.

funny thing.
before big, most people showed little interest in their dogs chasing me...
at least until i smacked their dog in the head with a rock.
now that big has joined me, people are all kinds of concerned about it.

"i bet he thought his christmas dog was dead meat, mr big."
i laughed.
big just walked on in silence.
big doesn't talk much, but he says a lot.

on the way back past that house, big left a new pee-mail.
i don't have much sense of smell, but i am pretty sure i know what it said;
"THIS IS BIG'S ROAD."

laz

01-04-13
the coyote hunters

i'm pretty sure we saw them before they saw us.

me and big were nearing the end of our walk
with the morning twilight just beginning to illuminate big
territory. we had been talking about the seasons.

i was bundled up against the morning chill
(big, of course, was loving the cold wind in his face)
winter solstice had officially arrived a few weeks ago,
but it never really feels like winter in these parts until january.

we had talked about how fall and spring seem to arrive on a
specific day, when me and big can feel it in our bones that the
season has changed.
but summer and winter sort of slide into place.
one day we just realize that the seasons have changed,
almost unnoticed.

we speculated on why the solar cycle does not match up exactly
with the seasons. logically, it would seem like the longest day of
the year would be the warmest, and the shortest day of the year
would be the coldest,
with the temperatures gradating between the two extremes
according to the length of the days.
instead, the longest and shortest days fall at the beginning of
warm and cold weather.

i tried to explain to big about the effects of ocean currents,
and the jet stream,
but i could tell i had lost him.
big was much more interested in:
where a racoon had crossed the road during the night,
a new fast-food sack in the ditch,
and the pickup truck slowly approaching.

the old truck was coming towards us in our lane,
so me and big switched sides of the road.
we not only know all the cars that we normally see in big
territory, but the times that we see them.

this strange vehicle,
at an odd hour, moving slowly;
piqued our interest.

since they had their lights on,
the men in the truck probably didn't see us until they had almost reached us.
the truck slowed to a stop,
and the driver greeted me;
"hi; i'm bob and this is john... we're coyote hunters."
"hey; i'm laz... and i'm walking."
(you look like coyote hunters, i thought)

about that time, big stood up on his hind legs to see who it was.
at the sight of big's massive head suddenly looking him in the eye, the coyote hunter drew back, startled.

"is that a good dog?"
"yeah, he's as good as they come."
i immediately regretted saying it.
i didn't know these two guys,
and i worry about my good-natured fella falling in the wrong hands.
the coyote hunter patted big's massive head,
and big wagged his tail

then he dropped to the ground to wait on us getting back to work.

"we're here to clean out the coyotes."
i had my doubts about that.
growing up out west, i was very familiar with coyotes.
they are smart and resourceful.
despite facing guns, poison, and traps
the coyotes flourished.
some places they were even hunted from airplanes.
the coyotes thrived in the face of it all.

coyotes had not even arrived in tennessee until the 1980's.
since that time, the most determined efforts had not "cleaned them out."
it had not even stopped them from spreading to every corner of the state.

the big year: winter and spring

me and big sometimes listen to the coyotes at night.
big smells where they have been while we are walking,
and sometimes we see their tracks in the snow or the mud.
once in a while we even spot one.
but we do not know where they stay.
coyotes are elusive.
i doubted that the coyote hunters would have much effect on the coyote population.
i could only hope they would not be shooting indiscriminately,
or scattering poison.

"where do you live?"
"down the road a ways."
that was as revealing as i cared to get with these two.
if the evasive answer bothered them, it didn't show.
"mr winston is letting us hunt on his property."
i just nodded.
"we can take care of the coyotes for you."
"they don't bother me."

"just don't forget that me and big are out before sunup a lot."

the coyote hunters went on their way.
me and big went on ours.

it is going to be an interesting winter in big territory.

01-06-13
the big question

big has been content to return to the bigloo now that the three weeks of daily rain have ended.
but i had come to like having him on the back porch at night.
there is a sense of security with big watching the house.
amy agrees.

sandra vehemently disagrees.
she thinks that if someone comes up to the house and big bites them (unlikely)
that the liability would wipe us out.
my thinking is that no one has any business coming up to our house between midnight and dawn.
especially out in the woods like we are.
if someone did, i would rather big was on the porch.

i know there are lawyers (even judges) on this list.
can i keep a big on the porch at night?

laz

01-07-13
harbingers of spring

coach big may love the cold,
and he has helped me develop a better attitude about it.
but my appreciation will never match his.
my general approach to 46 years of winter training has been to do it because it needs to be done...

and live for the harbingers of spring.

i start my spring-watch early.
winter solstice brings the first promise of spring,
and the coldest weather hasn't even started.
but those longer days...

those longer days will bring warmth eventually.

the planting of the winter wheat reminds me spring is coming.
that falls right around the solstice
(this year it was earlier)

right now the winter wheat looks like it is doing nothing,
the plants appear to be idly resting at a few inches tall.
but i know they are building the root systems that will support their later growth.
when those little plants take off,
warmer weather won't be far away.
i study them every day,
looking to see if they have grown any taller,
as if that will bring the warm weather sooner.

we are supposed to have a warm spell later this week.
i consider it the first early spring....
altho it differs from the last warm spell only by coming after the solstice.
that one i had considered as the final late fall.

but this morning had to have been the coldest day of the year (so far)
i hope it doesn't get any colder,
altho i know it probably will.

the big dog diaries

me and big got a good early start.
he was as happy as a big can be.
the cold weather inspired him to want to go faster
and he needed more than a few reminders not to pull.
what i noticed was that even in my warm christmas gloves
(possibly the best present i couldn't eat)
my fingertips were hurting.
my nose ached, and my moustache was stiff with ice.
i told coach big;
"forget about the harbingers of spring. i just want some harbingers of dawn!"
big didn't say anything.
"that sun is going to feel awful good this morning."
i knew what big was thinking.
"sun? we don't need no sun. what would feel good is a 30 mph wind, right in our faces!"
"i heard what you thought, you big goober. we don't need no wind, it's plenty cold already."

it was getting light while we passed thru the bottoms.
the coldest air likes to settle down in the bottoms and wait on the early runner.
my toes were almost as cold as my fingers.
now that it was light, i could see me and big's breath puffing out in big clouds of steam.
the sky had turned blue, so the sun had to be peeking over the hills, but i searched in vain for the first glimmer of light in the treetops.

just before we climbed out of the bottoms, a tiny chunk of ice hit my hat and ricocheted off into the road.
i watched it bounce on the pavement curiously,
then i looked up.
way up high, a flock of birds was passing over.
lucky birds.
they were in the sun.
one good thing about the coldest mornings.
bird poop freezes before it hits the ground...

or the early runner's hat.

the big year: winter and spring

we passed thru some long stretches of woods,
and finally we came around a bend where...
at the top of the rise ahead, in the very tops of the trees, i saw the first sunshine.

we got to the top of the climb with the saving grace of sunlight still way above us.
but there was hope.
i watched eagerly as we walked on,
and the sun, oh so slowly, crept nearer and nearer.

it was 3/4 of the way thru our "run" before we finally came out into a clear area,
passing between two pastures,
and the sun was there waiting for us.

it felt as good as i had expected.
training in the winter isn't all bad.

the rest of the way we were in and out of the sun.
we passed a spring, the "warm" springwater steaming as it left the ground,
forming a clear stream that fed into an ice-covered pond.
near the end we traveled alongside short creek.
i don't know why, but that stretch of short creek is always the coldest place anywhere around.

it was entirely tolerable, knowing when we turned and climbed back up out of the creek bottom,
a warm sun was waiting for us.

the day was a microcosm of winter training.
the cold is there. it bites at our extremities, and tries to burrow thru our layers of clothes.
but the promise of warmth awaits us on the other side.
even in the coldest places, on the coldest days, harbingers of spring are all around us;
like the rays of sunshine in the tops of trees.
we only have to stay the course until it arrives.

laz

ps. big's dog-food stealing nuthatch is back.
as i write this big is on the porch lying in the sun,
and his partially eaten bowl of food is sitting on the other side of
the porch in the shade.

from where i sit i can see the bowl, but i can't see big.
the nuthatch will fly up and land on the table....
and look and look at big's food bowl, and off where big is lying;
before finally flitting down to land on the side to try to reach in
and snag a pellet.
he's only there a fraction of a second before he takes off;
sometimes with a pellet, sometimes without.

big then leaps into the picture and stands over his bowl,
watching his nuthatch fly away.
after standing guard for a minute or two,
he exits stage left,
to return to his prime spot in the sun.

you can be sure his nuthatch is out in the woods watching.
waiting for those big eyes to close...

the show never gets old.

01-14-13
Every dog has his day

it had been "my day" for most of the past week.
even for tennessee,
january temperatures with lows in the 60's and highs in the 70's
is unusual.
if it wasn't for the fact that it rained most of the time,
it would have been darned pleasant.
as it was, we managed to hit the rain windows (weather radar is
a wonderful invention)
and altho we did get drenched a few times,
when i got greedy and tried to squeeze in too many miles,
it still was not unpleasant.

well, i didn't think it was unpleasant.
big huffed and puffed like it was midsummer.
he might not like warm weather,
but he was no less ready to go every day.
if our run didn't fall at the regularly scheduled time,
no problem for the big.
he is always ready to go.
anytime.
day or night.
he watched the rain like a hawk,
and made sure i knew every time it stopped.

last night that all changed.
tropical downpours and howling winds heralded the arrival of an
"arctic front"
i consider them as cruel gifts from our neighbors in canada;
raw, bitter cold air that cuts to the bone.
after readily acclimating to the balmy weather of the past week
it was a harsh shock to step out on the porch to visit with big
before bed.

as an aside, i figured out how to keep big on the porch at night.
sandra is a sleeping machine,
in bed long before i retire,
and still sleeping soundly long after i get up.
if i put big on his cable when i am gone during the day,

and don't mention his overnight whereabouts,
she is none the wiser.

to prove that i don't learn very fast, i was worried about the big.
however, he didn't seem in any way perturbed by the sudden change in temperature.
this morning when i came outside to get him,
i found that he was far from discomfitted by the cold wave.
big has two basic ways to greet a new day:
ecstatically happy, or a level above that.
this morning he was at the level above even that.
he met me with his tail wagging and his face lit up like it was christmas morning.
"look, look, it isn't raining!!!"
i felt the icy wind coming around the corner of the house...
it cut through my clothes and wrapped around my skin.
big ran out into the woods to pee,
and returned to the porch in two prodigious bounds.
i went back inside to bundle up in warmer clothes and check the weather radar.
sure enough there was no rain (or sleet or snow) on the screen.
but it was also 25 degrees, with a 10-15 mph north wind.
this would be fun.

big watched me adding layers through the window,
eyes shining and tail wagging a mile a minute.
when i picked up my boots he started drumming his front feet on the porch.
if you have a coach like big, you don't miss many days.
big wakes to a perfect day for running 365 days a year.

when i picked up his leash, he launched into a series of spontaneous leaps.
looking eye to eye into the big guy's silly grinning face,
as he passed by me at the zenith of each leap,
i almost could forget that we would soon be out of the relative shelter of the porch,
and fully exposed to the waiting canadian treat.

it wasn't too bad going down the hill on our south-facing driveway. nor did i have any real issue as we went around the bottom of the hill on the road.

the big year: winter and spring

but once we reached ben's hayfields, we were fully exposed to the wind.
i had to repeatedly remind big to stop pulling.
he was overjoyed that we had such a perfect morning.
"big. BIG! no need to pull. i am going to go as fast as i can."
(trust me, there would be no dawdling this morning!)

when he was learning about not pulling,
i used to tap the front of his outside ear with my trainer.
big never did like that.
so now, on mornings like this one, when he is simply too excited to listen,
i will slide the trainer up in my hand.
big can hear (or maybe sense) that motion.
he will duck his head and slow down immediately.

of course, the early part of the "run" is the worst.
i prefer to start into the wind, and finish with it at my back.
at least this day, i know the wind won't trick me by shifting at the midpoint, and blowing in my face all the way home as well.
big thinks the early part is the best.
he absolutely loves to walk head on into the wind.
the colder the better.

and this wind was a cold one.
the moisture seemed to lend it an extra cutting effect.
i had my layers well overlapped,
leaving no vulnerable points for the wind to slip its icy fingers inside. but i could feel the cold penetrating.

even my well-wrapped "man-bits" could feel the chill.
and my exposed cheeks and nose bore the brunt of the assault.

big was prancing around happily.
the past few days he had been focused in the 70 degree temperatures, head down, eyes straight ahead.
this morning he had his head up and wanted to investigate everything.

i bent my head into the wind,

trying to let my hood deflect some of it from my aching cheeks and stinging nose.

the only point on which we were in agreement;
let's go as fast as we can go.

we passed the trailer dogs.
the two long-haired dogs were curled into tight balls.
they barely looked up as we went past.
none of the normal come out and bark and act threatening routine.
the short haired trailer dog, the mean one, was nowhere to be seen. i suspect he was under the trailer pretending not to hear us going by.
not that he could have missed hearing us coming down the road;
"big. BIG! slow down. don't pull."

we went by without incident.
"see, big. even the long-haired dogs know it is cold this morning."
big answered by darting his nose into the tall grass,
and coming up with the still articulated lower jawbones of a deer.

he carried that proudly for a long way,
and it kept him busy trying to keep a grip.
when it finally slipped away, he begged to go back and get it.
"no big. you have plenty of bones at home. you don't need that one."

big didn't dwell on his loss for long.
we soon passed the carcass of a calf that had been hidden by the "hunter" who shot it.
as if the farmer would not know what had become of the calf...
i suppose the "hunter" hoped it would be blamed on coyotes.
it was the second such kill of the season.
"hey. it was brown, and it was moving. what was i supposed to do?"
always, ALWAYS wear orange during hunting season, people.

the vultures and coyotes had naturally found it almost immediately, and the half eaten remains were now in the middle of the road.
big was pretty sure that was something we should bring home.
"big. you cannot bring a dead calf home. now come on and forget about it."

the big year: winter and spring

i had to admit, the morning was pretty good.
big was having so much fun,
and big's fun is infectious.
none of the usual dogs pestered us
(this particular route usually features several dogs of the
nuisance variety)
and when we finally turned with the wind fully at our back for
the final mile...

it almost felt warm.

there was one final act to play out.
bigsprints.
we hadn't done any bigsprints during the week of warm weather.
big had just come home and plopped down.
he had some makeup work to do this morning.

he started early,
flying up the driveway as soon as we were in sight of the house,
whipping a tight turn around my car
and flying back to skid into a turn around me.
he got in multiple laps while i made my slow way up the drive.
and when i got close enough,
he started running in tight circles around my car,
leaned over at a 45 degree angle, a fantail of gravel flying out
behind him.
i laughed aloud.
"mr big. you're doing donuts!"
i passed the car, and he switched to doing different circles
out into the woods,
up onto the porch in two bounds,
back down in one humongous leap,
around the dog pen in another donut turn.
he went so fast, he ran so hard.
he defined the joy of living.
i climbed up the steps and just stood there watching him go.

he stopped as suddenly as he started.
two bounds up onto the porch and he executed the perfect
landing of an olympic gymnast,
stopping stock still without the slightest falter.
big looked at me, laughter in his eyes, panting heavily.

the big dog diaries

"are you ready to eat now, big guy?"
big trotted over and "SAT" in front of the table where his already
full food bowl was sitting.
(covered, to keep out the pellet-stealing nuthatch)

every dog has his day.
and today was big's day.

laz

01-25-13
the big goober

hello!
my name is big, and i am a goober.

i am not just any goober.
i am a "silly goober."

i am also a dog.
and not just any dog.
i am a "good dog."

i like being a good dog.
when i do what i am supposed to do
my master tells me i am a good dog.
and i can see he is happy.

i like to make my master happy.
that is my job.

yesterday i was a very good dog.
i know because my master told me.
every day we do our important work first.
master attaches my leash and we patrol our territory.
i have to be a good dog.
i am not supposed to pull
(that is hard)
i cannot chase squirrels and rabbits
(that is even harder)
i have to ignore barking dogs
(i am good at this, because master will take care of the dogs
if he needs to)

at the end of our walk master gets the mail.
(that is what he tells me he is doing)
and then i get to walk the rest of the way home without the leash.
i have to be twice as good,
because we are still doing important work.
yesterday a squirrel ran across the road, right under my nose.
it is hard not to chase a squirrel so close.
but i was still doing my work,

and i only watched him run.
master told me i was a "very good dog!"
i could tell he was proud of me.

it makes me feel good when i do right,
and master is proud of me.

one time i did not do right.
the new pug had found its way to our house
and i ran to see him.
he was afraid and ran off into the woods.
i followed him, even tho master called for me to stop.
i followed him a little ways,
and then i realized i must answer my master's call.
when i came back
master spoke to me harshly and did not pet me.
i felt very bad.

but master always forgives me.
in a little while he came back out and petted me.
now i am always a good dog.

but what i like most of all is to be a goober.
a silly goober.
at the end of our work master lets me run in the woods.
i have to stay close, but i can run as fast as i can run,
i can jump as high as i can jump,
and play as hard as i can play.
it feels good to run as fast and jump as high as i can.
and master laughs and tells me i am a silly goober.
i know when master laughs that he feels good too.
i like to make master feel good.
i run back and forth past master, and he laughs.
i spin in circles and he laughs harder.
i jump over bushes and briars and he laughs even harder.
and when i jump up as i go past, and look right in his eyes...

he laughs the hardest of all.
and tells me i am a silly goober.

it is a good thing to be a goober.

big

01-28-13
big providence

i wore my white tennis shoes when me & big went out this morning.
(by white tennis shoes, i mean tennis shoes which were originally white.)
it was kind of warm this morning and i like to alternate between shoes as much as possible.
in the recent string of cold-cold days
i had been wearing the same insulated shoes almost every day.

this morning i noticed immediately that the toe box of my white tennis shoes is kind of tight.
i noticed this because i had injured the little toe on my bad leg yesterday.
"tell you what, big; this is not going to be fun today."
big wagged his tail uncertainly.
he is a smart dog, but,
the idea that any day on the road could not be fun was beyond his comprehension.

about a half mile out i stopped and tried to adjust my shoe and sock to relieve the pressure.
it did not help at all.
"well big, i guess there is nothing to do but suck it up and go."
i focused on not limping.
there is nothing worse for you than favoring an injury.

it hurt like heck, and tears kept welling up in my eyes.
but we went on.
i figured it was an appropriate day to do the 5-mile minimum.

as we approached millersburg church i told big;
"i think we should turn around at the church, big guy."
turning at the church is actually 5 miles,
but we usually go another few hundred yards up to the top of a hill.
runners understand.
the top of a hill is a much better place to turn around.

and going a little over the designated distance just makes us feel righteous.

today i dreaded my toe hitting the end of the toe-box on the way back down.

we reached the church and big started the turn to go up the hill.
"you are right, big fella. what difference does one more hill make?"
so on we went.

after we started back, i saw a gray van (not intended as a insult to gray vans) approaching.
"dang, big. that's the second car today. traffic is crazy this morning."
the van started to slow, and i saw the drivers window going down.
nothing unusual about that, people are always stopping to say hello to big.
except this time i didn't recognize the vehicle.

it was an older lady, impeccably dressed, every hair perfectly in place.
she eyed big with cautious suspicion, but ambassador big always seems to know the situation.
he busied himself about sniffing her tires, to see what the dogs down her way had to say.
she spoke with a rich jawja accent,
old south dripped off of her words.
"ah think ah have made a wrong turn."
"can ya'll tell me how to get back to interstate 24?"

wrong turn hardly describes it.
how the heck did she get off the interstate and end up way out here??

"this road will take you there."
she was in luck. as long as she made no more turns she would eventually cross the interstate.
after that she had no choice but to parallel it until she came to an entry ramp...
even if she turned 180 degrees the wrong way, she would get back on the interstate.

even those directions required three repetitions.
she was clearly rattled.
and little wonder.
she had gotten off the interstate
(for what? to get gas? to use the powder room?)
and somehow ended up in the desolate middle of nowhere,
10 miles from any interstate.

as she started to go on she called out her window;
"y'all have a blessed day!"

me & big continued on our way.
"so what do you think, big?
i am pretty sure i know that lady.
i am betting southern baptist. old money.
i bet she has a handgun in her purse,
and calls black people 'colored'"

stopping to ask us for directions was probably the hardest
decision she had faced all month.
a grungy old man, in the middle of nowhere
faded and stained levis and blue jean jacket,
dirty orange sock hat...
and a 100 pound pit bull in tow
(with a head the size of a bowling ball)
she had to be desperate.

"you know what's really funny, mr big?"
big is always game to know what is really funny.
"if she had any idea how close we came to turning around at the
church....

if we'd made that turn, she would have never seen us.
she would have never seen anyone.
god only knows how much loster she would have gotten.
if she knew how we went just a little further for no reason at all,
she would have called it providence.
she would be absolutely certain god sent us to rescue her."

i have no doubt that she was praying before she found us.
i bet she sure didn't think we looked like the answer to a prayer.
we probably looked like her worst nightmare.

when she tells the story it will be;
"god works in mysterious ways!"

maybe it was my reward that my toe didn't hurt quite as bad the last mile or so home.
but i think the nerve pathway receptors were just already cloggged with pain messaging molecules.

i gotta try to do something with that toe.

laz

01-31-13
big decisions

"he has decided he belongs to you."

it seems like a lifetime ago that the vet told me that.
i had brought her this big, ugly, red dog.
this big scary-looking dog that had been shot in the chest.
i just wanted to see if he could be fixed.

he hadn't died on my porch like i expected when i brought him home.
he had probably decided he had to live because he belonged to me,
and i obviously needed a big, ugly, red dog to look after me.
after having him around for a day, there was no sending him off to be put down.
big has a way of winning your heart.

all i had in mind was to train him how to act in polite company, and then find him a good home.
big had decided he belonged to me.

when i read up on the breed,
i did make note that they were "strong willed."
they really need a stronger term.
at the time it didn't seem like his strong will would be such an issue.
his primary drive was clearly to please me.

but there were signs.
big decided that he did not belong in a pen.
and, by golly, no pen would hold him.
after finding out that, contrary to all previous experience, there was a dog that i could not contain,
we settled on a compromise.
he stayed on a cable in the back yard,
except when he wanted to unfasten it and come to the house.

the training went well.
big was a bright and willing student,
needing only a single repetition to learn any lesson.

the big dog diaries

we found him that good home; 300 miles away in st louis.
after experiencing life without a big for a few months,
i was not sad when he somehow found his way back.
maybe he was right. maybe i did need a big red dog.
but something had happened to my vision.
he didn't look so ugly any more.
other dogs looked too skinny,
and their heads were far too small.

big decided that it was his job to make sure i got my miles in every day.
if you have a big for a coach, you won't take many days off.
big has decided we need to go every day.

along the way i have come to understand what they meant by "strong willed."
big doesn't argue, he doesn't resist.
at least not actively.
but once he decides how something should be, he never forgets.
resisting the will of a big is like trying to hold back the tide.

big has decided that he should bring home the various rabbits and squirrels
that we find dead in the road during our morning walks.
he will give them up if i insist (and i always insist)
but he will still snatch up the next one we see, if he can.
i have learned not to let him walk too close to a road kill.
he just goes as close as his leash allows,
and tries to scoop them within reach of his mouth with his front paw.

the other day we came across a rabbit pancake.
i could see that it was flattened to a molecular thickness,
virtually welded into the road surface.
i figured it would be as hard to get off as a bumper sticker.
big, of course, knew it was there because he could "see" it with his nose.
foolishly i did not change course to go around it.
there was no way big could get that thing up without a scraper.

that was how i found out bigs have prehensile lips.
a quick dip of his head,
and big was walking alongside me carrying a rabbit pancake in

the big year: winter and spring

his mouth.
it made his already impossibly wide grin even bigger,
and he looked up at me, his eyes glowing with pride.
"you know you don't need that, don't you big guy?"
big is just a dog, and i know that.
so he can't understand english.
none the less, he didn't look at me again.

we walked along for a long time.
luckily he had picked up his rabbit pancake at the farthest end of our route.
i didn't have the heart to steal his prize,
so we just walked along that way.
actually, it made the walk easier.
we didn't have to stop to leave pee-mails.
the first time big found something worth stopping to sniff,
a chunk of rabbit pancake got scraped off.
he didn't do that again.
usually we have regular sudden stops,
when big comes across something interesting,
and i have to remind him;
"big, who is in charge of this expedition?"
i wondered what i would do when we got near the house.
at this point i didn't want to take away his treasure.

the problem was solved for me when we went past the home of the misfit pack.
they all came out for our usual greeting;
the tribbles tumbling all over each other as they ran in circles and yapped,
the fat white dog barking and kicking up a rooster tail,
and the queen just being in charge.
big looked at them with suspicion.
no doubt they wanted his rabbit pancake.
and just because they had never jumped the fence didn't mean they wouldn't.
big could clear it with ease,
if some foolish person were to tray and contain him inside.
i saw his jaws working,
and the protruding portion of his pancake disappeared right before my eyes.
then he pointed his nose up,

as he strained to swallow the mass of pulverized bone and hair.
in moments it was all over.
no one would be taking big's rabbit pancake now.

that's the big.

since big has decided that he belongs to me,
he has also decided that he should accompany me wherever i go.
he had been growing progressively more distressed every day
when i went to practice.
i might be going to the bank,
where the ladies pat his head and give him dog biscuits.
i could be going to the store or the post office.
each with a task for big to perform,
preferably one that included someone petting him.
he wasn't sure where i was going,
but i was going somewhere at the same time every day.
big decided he needed to go,
and i started finding that he had removed his cable
and was waiting by the car door when i came out to leave.

so one day i took him with me.
"you aren't going to enjoy this big. you can't go in."
indeed, big was not pleased to be left in the car.
he sat and watched the door that i went in,
until i came back out several hours later.
"see, big, this is not a fun trip."
the next day big was waiting by the car when i went out to go to practice.

so now practice is a regular thing.
big doesn't take his cable off anymore,
he waits on me to come and get him.
but he starts barking an hour in advance,
just to be sure i don't forget.
big does not believe in days off.

on the way to practice, he puts his elbow on the armrest,
and watches out the windshield.
once there, he doesn't have to look for me every second.
he likes to watch the people walk past.
sometimes he takes a nap.
if i so much as peek out through the cafeteria window,

the big year: winter and spring

his big head pops up, and he is looking at me.
how does he do that?

now big has decided that he needs to sleep on the porch at night.
maybe he thinks we need looking after.
he doesn't mind staying on his cable during the day. he sleeps on his chaise lounge in the sun,
dozes in the bigloo,
or plays one of his games.
but, when everyone goes to bed,
if i haven't let big up on the porch,
he lets himself off and comes on up.

sandra is not happy with this arrangement.
she accused me of letting the big "think he can just take off his cable and come up on the porch whenever he feels like it."

so i sternly commanded him to stay in his bigloo the next night.
and he did so for a few days....

until about 5 in the morning one day when i hadn't come get him on time.
he barked and barked,
and when i didn't come get him...

he took off his cable and came to get me.
sandra just doesn't seem to understand
when my explanation for something he does begins with;
"well, big has decided...."
she always cuts me off with;
"HE IS A DOG! you are the human. WHO IS IN CHARGE?"

she ought to just be glad he didn't decide that she "owns" him.

laz

02-02-13
the big snow

today started like so many others,
turning the tv on to weather radar in a dark living room.

when the picture came on, there was something new.
we were right in front of the leading edge of a 100 mile wide band of purple...

sleet. freezing rain.

i'm not sure about other people, but sleet is not my favorite.
sleet or no sleet, when i looked outside into the half-light,
there was big's hopeful face in the window.
"you know big, it's gonna sleet."
big wagged his tail and bobbed his head with excitement.
"yeah, you're right. it's frozen. maybe it'll just bounce right off us."
why bother arguing?
if you have a coach big, you don't take many days off.

we walked into the growing light for much longer than i expected with no precipitation at all.
the whole valley seemed to be cloaked in a calm silence.
our walking sounds were magnified by the stillness.
we heard turkeys gobbling a couple of times.
and once, the harsh, accusing call of a blue jay seemed to rend the heavy air.
i had started to wonder what happened to the weather
when a slight breeze began to blow into our faces from the east.
the wind always brings you something.
the south wind brings rain, the north wind brings cold, the west wind brings storms...

and the east wind brings change.
i looked overhead to see the solid line of that big winter weather front directly overhead,
moving from west to east.
the east wind would be the ground layer of air being rolled under, as the incoming front went over the top of it.

it was really quite impressive.
half the sky light, half of it slate gray.
divided by a line from horizon to horizon.
the leading edge was roiling like a wave on the beach,
but behind it was just a solid dull gray.
my dad used to call them snow clouds.
from what the weather radar said, they would be sleet clouds.

me and big walked on while the sleet cloud raced ahead and soon covered the entire sky.
"i understand why it is so quiet when it snows, big. i think the snow absorbs the sound.
but why is it so quiet now?
do all the animals have weather radar and know what is coming?"
big wasn't giving away any animal secrets today.

a little later i saw a single snowflake fluttering to the ground in front of us.
"look big guy, a snowflake. that's not sleet."
big was more interested in leaving a pee-mail.
i bet he was warning the animals to keep their weather radar hidden.

a minute later we saw another flake,
then another, and another.
pretty soon we were in a regular light snow.
as cold as it had been the past couple of days,
the road surface was soon partially obscured by patches of white.
snow collected on big's broad back,
formed into clumps, and then fell off in miniature avalanches.
i told big;
"this ain't sleet, but i ain't complaining"
me and big love walking in the snow.

as we passed by the trailer,
i saw the black trailer dog slinking off into the woods with something in his mouth.
it was a dead skunk.
the two white trailer dogs were nowhere to be seen.
i haven't seen anyone at the trailer in several weeks,
and am beginning to wonder if the trailer dogs have been

the big year: winter and spring

abandoned.
the black trailer dog is looking very thin,
and they have been dragging up various carrion and eating it.

a little later we spotted the two white trailer dogs eating
something on the side of the road.
when we got close, they also slunk off into the woods.
i couldn't tell for sure what they had been eating,
all that remained was an inside out skin and four feet.
the feet looked suspiciously like they belonged to a housecat.
"i gotta call ben when we get home, mr big, and see if he knows
what is going on at the trailer."
if the dogs have been abandoned and take to eating people's pets,
something will need to be done.

an hour into our workout, the snow was coming down hard and
heavy.
big flakes filled the air and the road was soon covered
completely.
big slowed down until he was walking right beside me,
and i could see the snow was heaping up on his nose until it was
about to obscure his vision.

then big gave a mighty shake, and snow sprayed off him in all
directions.
for the next minute, the big red dog stood out in contrast to the
whiteness all around,
then the snow was once again accumulating on his back and
head.

it didn't take long before we were walking in a half inch of snow.
then an inch.
we stopped at the top af a long uphill straightaway and looked
back.
there was me and big's footprints,
side by side, right down the middle of the road,
all the way back until they were too far away to make out.
ours were the only tracks.

we came to a fresh set of rabbit tracks crossing the road.
they meandered slowly to the middle, then stopped...

before taking long straight leaps off into the bushes.
"that's where he heard us coming, big fella."
big was snuffling away.
for once i knew as much as he did.

not long after the rabbit tracks,
the snow started to dwindle,
the flakes growing smaller and smaller
before being replaced by pinhead sized balls of ice.
at the same time, the calm ended,
and a steady wind began blowing in our faces,
driving the ice pellets into us.
the sleet stung my cheeks and i was glad that i was wearing glasses. i looked at big and i could see him blinking as the pellets struck his eyes.
"that icebreaker head isn't so effective against sleet, is it big fella?"
big's answer was to start pulling insistently.
he wasn't having fun anymore, he was ready to head home.

lashed by the wind-driven sleet,
there was no discouraging big from pulling,
until we reached the final turn on the way home.
there is a short, steep drop between the turn and short creek bridge, and when i stepped on the steep slope and big gave an unexpectedly strong tug,
my feet went out from under me on the inch-deep,
ice-coated snow
and i landed with a thud and a curse;
"big, you idiot! that's why i don't want you to pull."

maybe it was because we had turned the stinging, ice-filled wind out of our faces.
maybe it was because big felt bad about pulling me down,
whatever the reason, there would be no more pulling...
at least for today.

we did have another hassle at the short creek kids' house.
the new family has a small, friendly pit bull,
and she wants to come out and play with big every time we pass.
friendly dogs are the hardest ones to deal with.
she wants to play a game called;

the big year: winter and spring

"run in circles around the man holding the leash"
big wants to play, too.
but he is on the other end of the leash.
i think the human version of that game is called tetherball, or maybe maypole...

and i am the maypole.

the best i can muster are some halfhearted slaps on her flank with my trainer.
i just lack the will to smack a friendly dog.
friendly dogs are the hardest to deal with.

nature versus nurture?
this happy, friendly dog with a shoebox for a head
is almost a dead ringer for the insane pit bull that rages at the end of a chain at the pug house.
she is slightly smaller,
and her spots are tan instead of chestnut colored.
when she is out, we have a laughing hassle until (to my relief) she turns back for home.
if the insane pitbull ever gets off his chain,
i assume me and big will have to kill him,
and hope we don't get seriously injured in the process.
i remember when the insane pit bull was a friendly puppy.
i have watched while he lost his mind, out on that chain.
the difference in those dogs is nurture.

the insane pit bull didn't see us today.
he was watching a couple of elementary school age kids sledding in the snow.
they were probably 7 or 8 years old.
i heard one of them say;
"don't run over that cat."
the other one answered;
"we have too many fxxxing cats anyway."
nature versus nurture.
who knows?

there was one last act to go,
and i could see big was eager.
he was nearly quivering in anticipation.
i didn't have to check the mailbox...

45

there were no tire tracks on our road yet,
so i turned into the driveway and asked;
"would you like to play off leash a little bit, bigness?"
big's answer was to stop dead in his tracks.
he remained motionless until i unhooked the leash and said;
"OK"
then he was off like a shot,
snow exploding from under his feet at every stride, he tore up the drive,
executed a screaming 180 and came back at me,
like a grinning locomotive,
that round face alight with pleasure,
he cut around me in a ridiculously tight turn,
snow and gravel spraying from under his huge feet,
and was off again.
all the way up the driveway bigsprints were in full swing.
he would weave thru the woods at full speed,
with cuts and turns that an nfl running back would envy.
up and down the driveway
with bursts of speed that would leave usain bolt agog.
i wondered if big doesn't get 90% of his actual exercise in that last 5 minutes coming up the drive.

the last act is the traditional circling of my car.
big must keep a bone there, just for that purpose.
he cuts an impossibly fast and tight donut around my car,
flips his bone into the air,
and then does another.
he can do it 4 or 5 times before i get there.
amy came out on the porch to watch the show.
you can't miss when me and big get home;
between his thundering feet, and my laughter and cheers.

his outer fur was pretty well soaked,
so we didn't finish with a lot of petting today.
i didn't want to push the moisture into the underfur that keeps my big guy warm.
he just ate some breakfast and settled for a little chest scratching.
then i went to the end of the porch and looked to check out the bigloo.
it sat there in deep snow,
the remnants of his last tarp draped over it.

"looks prettty crappy out there, big fella. maybe i can let you take a nap on the porch for now."
i turned around to see that big was already in his bed in the corner, looking at me hopefully.
"OK big. you can stay there for now."
big got up and was busy fashioning himself a cozy nest as i went inside."

laz

02-05-13
requiem for the trailer dogs

it isn't just cats and skunks.
big hates racoons.

sometimes when big is sniffing at animal crossings,
he will get really intense and
that 4-inch wide strip of hair down his back will stand on end.
i have always wondered what animal it was that aroused such hostility.
i thought it might be cats or skunks.
(altho it is generally pretty easy to tell when a skunk has been by)
i had speculated about coyotes...
altho when i saw coyote sign,
he generally acted much like he does for strange dogs.

yesterday the question was answered.
racoons are an animal that i don't see very often.
not only are they nocturnal,
they are very discreet.
those i have seen have mostly been at some distance,
and big has not spotted them.
his vantage point is too low.

but me and big are pretty quiet for the most part,
and yesterday we came upon a racoon crossing the road right at daybreak.
he must have been late on his way to one of his dens for spending the day.
he was about 20 yards upwind, trundling along in no particular hurry. big was sniffing the air, and i could see his hackles raising.

they must have sensed each other,
because the racoon suddenly stopped and looked around, right at us. at the same time, big raised his head and spotted the coon.
they both froze (and me with them)
the only thing that moved was the 4-inch bristling mohawk that stood up down big's back.
we all stood that way for what felt like a long time.

maybe it was only a few seconds.
then bedlam broke loose.
the racoon took off into the woods, running for its life.
big hit the end of his leash like a freight train.
lucky for me i have plenty enough ballast to stop a speeding big.
the racoon was long gone out of sight before i got big to settle down.

then, when we crossed the racoon's trail,
i had to start all over.
big wanted to go after the varmint,
but he finally had to settle for leaving a pee-mail.
i think i know what it said;
"this is big's road."
"NO CATS OR SKUNKS OR RACOONS ALLOWED!"

and he has been doing better with cats.
while he is still far too interested in any felines we see,
he stays pretty much under control...

unless they walk on his road.

when you are a number one dog, you have to set *some* rules.

the racoon was not the only new thing we saw yesterday.
but the next time it was my turn to be unhappy.
we came to a creek, and there was a dead calf laying on the bank.
a little further down the road, at the next creek,
there were two dead calves in the water.
then two in a ditch,
and finally another one in short creek, itself.
someone had decided that our little valley was the ideal place to dispose of cow carcasses.

i called the county when i got home.
i wasn't sure what department was in charge of dead cows,
but it turned out to be animal control.
i felt pretty sorry for the guy who had to drag all those dead cows out of the creeks.
me and big were out again when he came by,
and he stopped to talk.
all the cows' ear tags had been removed,

the big year: winter and spring

so that the culprit could not be identified.
but he was asking around at nearby farms with cattle...

and anyone he saw out walking.

i owned up to being the one who had called in,
and he expressed appreciation, instead of being unhappy.
the cows would have been a lot more unpleasant to remove later on, and it is unacceptable to dump animal carcasses into creeks.

we talked a little longer,
and i told him i might be calling again later on,
that there were some dogs we thought might be abandoned.
turns out, someone had already called to report abandoned dogs at a trailer,
they just hadn't specified exactly where the trailer was.
and everyone's dogs run loose around here.
i told him i would monitor the situation,
but he wanted to go and check on the dogs himself.

this morning when big and i walked past the trailer,
there were no trailer dogs.
that didn't give me a good feeling,
so this afternoon me and little went by again,
from the other direction.
still no trailer dogs.
funny, but after years of having them growling and barking and threatening me, it seemed lonesome and quiet without them.

from this direction i could see a paper taped to the side of the trailer. i hesitated; having never set foot in that yard,
but curiosity got the better of me.
i walked just a few steps inside the gate, so i could read the large print.
the heading was "Pet Welfare and Adoption"
and i could see a handwritten line saying "Call 999-9999 about your dogs immediately"
i looked around.
the trailer looked abandoned in the best of times.
today it looked positively desolate without even the trailer dogs around. there was no new trash in the midden heap
and the area around the gate was littered with the bones of animals the dogs had eaten.

51

thinking about it, the black dog had been let off his chain about the same time i stopped seeing people.
i wondered if they had at least had the concern to let him loose and give him some chance of foraging for himself before abandoning all the dogs.

it was a sad walk home.
it has been from yesterday morning until this afternoon,
essentially two days and still the paper is up.
those dogs have been abandoned.
the black dog and the white dog are older dogs,
and not exactly lovable.
no one is going to take them home.
the "pup" has never been outright hostile.
but it is a full grown dog and somewhat feral.
"those dogs were not as lucky as you, little."
little did not say anything.
she is not as wise as big.
but sometimes she is a little wise.

am i wrong to hope that the next time me and big or little walk past the trailer,
there are 3 ill-tempered dogs there;
barking and growling, and threatening to bite me,
while i brandish my trainer and threaten to knock their teeth out?

laz

02-10-13
trailer dogs, the final story

first the big news.
using some donations from big's friends
i bought him a pretty yellow canvas tarp,
along with some heavier rope to hang it with.
(canvas tarps are really heavy)

yesterday was finally a sunny day without much wind,
so i put it up for him.
big was the only one helping,
and to be honest, he wasn't that helpful.
i think if he was more than 2 feet tall at the shoulder,
he might have been more help.
whether he was a big help or not,
he had a big time helping.

once i got it up, me and big surveyed the result.
it wasn't near as high as i wanted,
but i plan to re-hang it when someone taller than big
(and perhaps sporting opposable thumbs)
is here to help.

i told big;
"it looks pretty good right now. but we won't know for sure until it goes thru some weather."
big just wagged his tail and grinned up at me.
i knew what he was thinking.
over the past 3 years we have had a storm within 24 hours every single time i have hung him a new tarp.
most of them have demolished his latest shelter.

sure enough, by last night they were issuing wind warnings for this morning.

the tarp held.
not only did it suffer no damage,
it is still hanging just the way i put it up.
so big is back in business.

now for the trailer dogs.

the big dog diaries

i cannot explain why i felt sorry for the trailer dogs.
for three years they have been a nuisance every time i went by.
after their first encounter with my trainer they kept a safe
distance, but they still had to be watched.
our relationship was that they threatened to bite me,
and i threatened to knock out their teeth.

it was no problem with big,
he has learned to ignore dogs and let me deal with them.
little is a typical terrier....
either fearless or brainless (maybe both)
she tries to attack any strange dog,
or even group of dogs,
without regard to their size or numerical advantages.

dealing with dogs is only complicated by little lunging and
issuing her war cry,
or running in circles around my legs.

the trailer dogs were such a nuisance that i thought i would be
glad they were gone. instead, i found myself distressed at the
thought of them being put down.

every day the animal control notice wasn't removed,
i got more stressed.
i felt like i should do something.
i started asking neighbors if they knew how to reach the lady
who lives in the trailer.

i was amazed to find out that she has been here for years,
and no one knows her name.

no one knows her name,
but everyone has heard the rumor she "has cancer."
neither can anyone remember who told them she "has cancer."

we all know she has a grown daughter with 2 kids,
because just during the 3 years i have lived out here,
the daughter and kids have come to live with her 3 or 4 times,
for periods ranging from a few weeks to 6 months.

and everyone knows about her son.
he is notorious for tearing up peoples' yards and fields with his

the big year: winter and spring

4-wheel drive truck.
one neighbor assured me that he would also "steal anything he can get his hands on."

so after 4 days, the notice disappeared.
the son had come and took it down,
i knew because he had left tell-tale trenches in neighboring properties with his truck.

that should have made me feel better.
now that the owners knew, what happened next was up to them.
instead a new narrative started in my head.
that poor woman was in the hospital with cancer,
and she had left her son to;
"look after the dogs"
which he took to mean "check on them about once a week"
while he was out tearing up property with his truck
(and possibly looking for something to steal)
he might have just taken down the notice so he could tell his mother;"i don't know what happened to them?"

i had nothing against the woman.
every time i have seen her outside she has apologized for her dogs, which would come after me with greater vigor,
either emboldened by their master's presence,
or trying to prove their worth.

i finally called animal control to ask what became of the trailer dogs.

well, he reclaimed the two older dogs,
and left the young one.
that was the lucky one.
it is only about a year old,
and has not yet developed a nasty disposition.
and animal control,
which generously labeled the dog a "pyrrhenies"
says there is a "friends of pyrrhenies" shelter that will take it,
if it is not adopted.

the other two are now chained up outside the trailer.
each has now got a "shelter"
consisting of some plywood scraps nailed together

to make a 3-sided shelter with a roof.
they aren't but barely big enough for the dogs,
but it is more than they had.

and each dog has a shiny new "water bowl"
an aluminum pan that ought to hold more than a gallon of water.
i hope the son plans to check on them more than once a week.

me and big need to plan our runs to go past the trailer about
every day, at least for a while.

laz

02-11-13
the white trailer dog makes a break for it

i appreciate everyone's concern for the trailer dogs.
but i cannot take on the responsibility of caring for them.
the best i can do is monitor their situation,
and make sure they do not come to a bad end....

that task got simpler this morning,
the white trailer dog is gone.

me and big decided she probably escaped,
and is trying to make her way back to the animal shelter...

known to the trailer dogs as "heaven on earth."

i don't know why she decided to leave; she had the good shelter.
hers has 3 walls and a roof.
the black dog just has several pieces of plywood and sheet metal
leaned together like a teepee.

i am reminded of the great horse barn project.
somehow the trailer folks came by 3 ponies last spring.
they have about a 1 acre field next to the trailer,
and one day there were 3 ponies and a big round bale of hay
there.

then they built a horse barn....
actually it was four upright cedar poles,
with three walls and a roof made from scraps of plywood and
sheet metal
and a dirt floor.

after about a month, the roof fell down inside the barn.
then they had 3 walls and a floor made of scraps of sheet metal
and plywood.

the ponies were gone before christmas,
by which time one of the walls had fallen down.
the remaining two walls are still standing, amidst a huge
weedbed.

me and big make bets every time we walk that way,
over which wall comes down next.

laz

02-12-13
the big catastrophe

i was pretty mad at the big this morning...

at least i tried to be.
it is hard to be mad,
when he comes out, tail wagging,
that funny-looking, squat, muscular body fairly wriggling with pleasure,
looks up at you with those big, shining, adoring eyes,
and leans against your legs looking for affection.

"you are a goober, big."
"you have got yourself in a mess, and i don't know how i am gonna fix it."
big's only answer was to moan with pleasure, nearly shut his eyes, and wag even harder.
i think my "scolding" would have been more effective is i wasn't rubbing the broad top of his head.

mad or not, there was a real problem.
my silly dog had wrought another big catastrophe yesterday,
and i wasn't sure how, or even if, i could fix it.

but, i should tell this story from the beginning.

out loss on saturday was not enough to end my basketball responsibilities.
i had an obligation to continue going to our girls' games,
as long as they could last.
and i needed to attend the other boys games through the district tournament, because there would be the voting for the stupid "all tournament" team at the end.
heck, i would even have to be there for our guys after the finals because they hand out the regular season awards at the same time.

i hate the awards and the awards ceremonies.
i never stay for them,
except when i am a coach on one of the teams.
then i have no choice.

i always tell my players that;
"the least important thing you will get from basketball is individual awards."
i have seen players sacrifice the team's interest in an effort to be all-district or maybe even mvp,
and i have seen good teams ripped assunder by the distribution of trophies.
many a team has stumbled in the region from the after-effects of the district tournament all-star picks.

none of that mattered. i had to go.

so i left yesterday afternoon.
before i went, i checked on all the dogs.
sophie and little were easy enough.
sophie was in the pen, and i told little to "STAY" on the porch.
little is pretty reliable,
she would only leave the porch to use the bathroom,
or if amy came home before i did.
big was reclining in the sun on his chaise lounge
(a beloved big possession)
his bright yellow tarp hung over his bigloo,
providing shelter if he should need it.
his supper was going to be really late tonight,
and i briefly wondered if he might take off his cable.
sandra would be mad if he came out to meet us.
he had gotten to taking it off every day,
but since i seriously scolded him for it a couple of weeks ago,
he had been good about staying on it until i came and got him...

the way things turned out,
i wish he had just taken off his dadgum cable.

when i got home about 2300 hours,
the first thing i heard was big's "help me" bark.
so i knew something was up,
but at least he had stayed on his cable.

as i walked around the corner of the house,
the first thing i saw in the darkness was the light shadow of his tarp. i knew immediately that it was not hanging right.
i couldn't see the big,

the big year: winter and spring

but i could hear him "wooo, wooo, wooo"
he was going to be rescued.

getting closer, i could tell that his tarp was hanging straight
down to the ground.
somehow, the back end had come loose.
a freak gust of wind?
no, that couldn't be right.
it had gone through gale force winds yesterday, unscathed.
big's problem was easy to diagnose.
the tarp was laying across the top of his bigloo,
and hanging over the door.
he couldn't get inside to sleep.

as i pulled the tarp back over the house
i discovered disaster.
the right rear corner grommet was gone.
that was bad, but the left side was worse.
much worse.
the left rear corner grommet was still attached to the tree.
the double-thickness border was still intact,
hanging all the way to the front....

in a long 2-inch wide strip.

the tarp itself had been ripped away,
all the way from the back to the front.
big's wonderful, expensive tarp had been totally destroyed.

i thought about some impossible weather event.
i considered the possiblity of a vandal with a knife.
nope.
this had to be big.
but how?
i would have to wait until daylight to find out.

the story was easy enough to decipher the next morning.
it would not have required an indian scout to figure out.
big's tracks told the tale.
with all the recent rain,
there was a lot of mud at the back of his area,
and he had not been going back there.
a single set of tracks followed the former boundary of the tarp;

back along the left side (where the border still hang)
then turned at a right angle to follow along the back,
and just around the right corner.
i could picture big walking along,
and looking up at the edge of his tarp...
wheels turning in that big head of his.

the right rear corner was tied a little lower than the rest,
so that rain would run off.
that was the weakness big must have been looking for,
because i could see where he had stopped.

then his rear feet had dug deeply into the ground when he leaped
up impossibly high in the air,
to clamp down on the tarp.
who needs a dog that can jump 6 feet in the air?
the rope and grommet were nowhere to be seen,
i figured that when his free-falling big weight had hit the corner
of the tarp,
that grommet must have shot off like a bullet...

i looked around, and sure enough there was the grommet,
still attached to the rope,
laying at the base of the tree where the rope was tied off.

if i needed any more proof what had happened,
about 4 inches up from the corner,
a flap of the tarp had torn out,
just the size of a big mouth.

there were no circling tracks,
no chaos of repeated leaps.
he had brought down the tarp on the first try.
i looked down at big, wagging his tail and grinning back at me.
"you are one smart idiot, big. now what are you going to do when it rains?"
"i wish you had just taken off your darn cable."

having secured one corner of the tarp,
big then turned and began pulling the back of the tarp to the front.
after it had folded under all the way to the other corner,
he just kept pulling until it ripped thru the border,

the big year: winter and spring

and then ripped all the way up the side.
what a pleasing sound that must have made....

rrrrrrrrrrrrrrrippppppppp

i am surprised that the other grommet did not also pop out,
but the twist in the canvas where it was folding under must have concentrated the force.
i would be surprised that he could exert enough force to rip through the double thickness, double stitched border of the tarp...

but i have seen video of bigs pulling sleds with tons of weight.
they are incredibly strong blocks of muscle.

my first thought was that i could not put up a new tarp until i had help to get it extra high.
the second thought was that big is screwed.
his big funds are depleted.
heartworm medicine, tarps, a new cable every few months,
and food (big is like feeding a new holland hay baler)
it costs more to keep up a big than it does me.

"well, mr big. you know the other dogs don't have tarps up over their houses."
"you are about to experience how the other half lives."

big just wagged his tail,
and i think he might have looked just a little proud of himself.

it took longer to take down the remnants of his tarp,
fold it up and coil the ropes,
than it did to set the whole thing up.

"one good thing."
i told the bigness;
"the tarp is destroyed for a big shelter,
but it will be good for covering the barkley chicken."

i warned the big that when today's rain gets here,
he will just have to tough it out in the bigloo.

he is waiting for the rain to start,
cozy in his back porch bed.

he is like a small child.
affectionate, friendly, and sometimes destructive...

in the most fun loving, non-malicious manner.

and who could leave their child out in the rain?
even if i am trying to be mad at him.

laz

02-18-13
puppy love

big was so excited to see me yesterday
that he did a flip.

it had been a while since i was greeted with a flip.
good old big doesn't do as many flips these days.
it was just another reminder that my big buddy isn't as young as he used to be.

there is a myth that dog years have a human year equivalency.
each dog year being the same as 7 human years.
this is, of course, somewhat, but not exactly true.
dogs have a much more compressed childhood and adolescence,
such that the first year of a dog's life is more like 18 human years.
the pace slows some in the second year,
but a two year old dog is still more like a 25 year old human, physically.
after the first two years it does settle in,
with an average dog burning thru the rest of their lives at about 5 years to one.
bigger breeds typically aging a little faster than that,
small dogs sometimes slower.

emotionally, it is a different story.
dogs seem to stop at about the level of a 3-year old,
living out their lives emotionally needy,
worshipping their masters and wanting to be close.

at somewhere between 4 and 4.5 years old,
i can see my big friend passing thru familiar stages of life.
while he is still a phenomenal athlete,
he has lost a step.
it happens to all of us by the time we reach the latter half of our 30's.

just the other day i saw big come up short on one of his most amazing leaps.
he usually bounds up the steps to the porch in two steps,
skipping over both flights, and just hitting the landing in the

middle.
when he was really cranked up doing his bigsprints,
sometimes he would literally fly all the way from the ground to
the porch in one incredible leap,
covering 18 or 20 horizontal feet, and 5 vertical feet in a single
bound.

it was bitterly cold,
and big was tearing about in ecstacy,
as he is wont to do at the end of our morning walks
(especially on wonderfully cold mornings)
as i approached the porch,
big swung around in one last furious circle thru the woods,
and came at the porch head on just ahead of me.
as always, it was the most improbable sight;
his stocky body seeming to float thru the air as he sailed towards
the porch,
front feet stretched out ahead of him.

but the outcome that day was different.
instead of his front feet landing on the porch and his back feet
landing right behind them,
as he stuck a motionless landing that any olympic gymnast
would die for, his front feet came up inches short, and caught the
front of the last step.
the big guy hit the porch on his chest and chin,
and slid all the way to the back door.

he was clearly shaken by the impact.
another thing that happens to us as we get older is that we don't
bounce back up like we used to.
so i told big the story of my last "dunk."
in my early 20's i could dunk.
only by the narrowest of margins,
but like any young male it was a point of great pride.
as i got older my life changed,
and eventually i didn't play basketball anymore.
one day when i was in my late 30's
"about the age you are now, big guy"
i was walking down the basketball court carrying a basketball
after a practice,
and it popped into my head to dunk it.

the big year: winter and spring

this kind of idea can happen to a man at any age.
i blame it on testosterone inhibiting brain function.
i got a short running start, sprang off the floor, gave the classic knee punch to gain extra elevation,
and soared towards the goal.

it felt like the same jump i used to make,
but the similarity ended there.
almost immediately, i knew i was not going to get the ball high enough to dunk.
briefly i was struck with fear that i would catch the front of the rim with the ball.
when you can only dunk by the narrow margin i could dunk by, you know all about catching the front of the rim with the ball.
your upper body stops, your feet keep going, and you hit the floor on your back like....

well, as amy says, like a sack of feed corn.

at 21 it hurts, but it is funny.
at 39 i wasn't sure if i would ever get back up.

my fears were unfounded;
i sailed past well beneath the front of the rim.
the ball didn't even clip the net.

me and big talked a lot about this aging thing while we walked this morning.
he isn't the crazy pup he used to be.
he often enters his bigloo walking these days,
rather than hitting it like a runaway locomotive.
sometimes he goes up the back steps, and hits every step...

and he only does flips on special occasions.

i told him i wasn't crazy about him aging right before my eyes.
on the other hand, there wasn't any other way to get where we are now.
it was fun when he was still a young pup,
but not as satisfying as the relationship we have developed.
in a way we are like an old married couple.
not a lot of surprises left,
but we have learned how to work together pretty well.

we are familiar and comfortable,
and we rely on each other.

big didn't say anything.
but the big has a way of teaching me things without saying anything.
he lets me work them out for myself.
he started to angle over in front of me,
his attention on a flattened ketchup pack in the middle of the road.
in a second i was going to step on his heel, so i clicked my tongue.
big eased back over into his proper position.

i told big we were pretty lucky.
look at all those other dogs we see every day.
they are the center of attention when they are puppies,
then their masters grow bored with them when they are dogs.
and everyone loses,
dogs aren't kids, that grow up and have their own lives.
emotionally the dog is always a three year old.
old dogs need the attention just as much as puppies do.
the bored masters lose out just as much.
puppies are cute, and they are fun.
but that is no match for the satisfaction of working with a good experienced dog.

thinking i had gotten big's lesson, i told him;
"everybody loves a puppy. it's just that a lot of them don't love the dog."

boom. it struck me like a lightning bolt. "puppy love."
when i was a kid i was told that puppy love was when you were young, and didn't know what love really was...
like a puppy.

that isn't it at all.
puppy love isn't about how young you are.
it is loving the newness, not the object.
it is the love everyone has for a puppy,
that too seldom develops into a love for the dog.
me and big see the residue of puppy love every day.
the pug house people would probably tell you they "love dogs."
god knows they have enough of them.

the big year: winter and spring

they are just stuck at the stage of puppy love.
i remember when the insane pit bull was a beloved puppy,
and they doted on him.
he was with someone every second.
then one day he was a dog, and they lost interest
and chained him in the yard to slowly lose his mind.
there have been two more puppies since then.
each meeting the same fate.
at least they chained the insane pit bull,
all the other jilted lovers have been left outside to run loose,
and become threatening nuisances to anyone who passes.

puppy love is what happens to the short-timers in the ultra
world (remember, i promised ultra content)
they love the newness.
they love being an "ultrarunner."
but if the dog love of ultrarunning itself never develops,
the sport demands too much for the runner to last.
ultras end up out in the yard,
with all the other abandoned hobbies.

by this time, me and big had reached the driveway.
"too heavy today, big guy. tomorrow lets just talk about rabbits"
we started up the driveway,
and i let him off his leash so he could play in the woods.
about halfway up the hill, i noticed something different in the
way he held his head.
i knew my big friend had spotted something off in the woods.
i watched him closely, and sure enough he started to take off
after whatever it was;
"STOP!"
big froze, but continued to stare intently.
his hackles were bristling.
"you better just stay here with me, big fella."
big looked for another few seconds,
then he seemed to shrug,
and turned to come back and walk beside me.

puppies are fun. but nothing beats a good dog.

laz

02-23-13
terror in bigistan

big's love of cold weather never fails to amaze me.
the last few days have been among the coldest of the winter,
starting in the low teens, with a cruel north wind chilling me to the bone.
looking at big out in his clearing,
lying on his chaise lounge,
the freezing wind whipping across the barren ground,
i was reminded of the kyrgyz, tajiks, and other inhabitants of the high plateaus and mountains of central asia.
big's area has needed a name,
so i dubbed it bigistan.

me and big had established a new routine.
after we did our morning walk, he was more than happy to go to bigistan for the day.
he spends his days lounging in the sun
either napping or surveying the wooded hillsides.
suppertime is 1630,
so i can count on big giving me advance warning by 1600.
about 1615 i can count on seeing him come bouncing up the steps to the back porch,
having saved me the trouble of coming to remove his cable.

after supper, big is glad enough to go back to bigistan,
but sometime in the evening,
if i don't come and get him,
he unfastens his cable and comes up to spend the night in his bed next to the back door.

it is the great unspoken not-quite-secret.

big is a sight to see, heading out on these cold mornings.
he seems to be up on his tippy toes,
head bobbing with every enthusiastic step, funny bat-wing ears bouncing.
all i can do is bundle up, and pull my hood as tight as i can get it.
if big wasn't having so much fun these would be hard mornings to get myself out.

this morning was different.
it got up to 50 yesterday, and started raining.
it rained all night and stayed around 50.

me and big were all over the weather radar,
and we were out right behind the last drops of rain.
we were so tight on the heels of the rain
that we got past the pug house unnoticed.

but the day that started so well ended much more ominously.
as me and big were going around the last curve before the driveway,
a caravan of no fewer than six big trucks and suv's went past us.

now, any strange vehicle on our road draws attention.
but six vehicles is a week's worth of traffic.
neither me nor big could imagine what all those vehicles would be doing out here.
i didn't tell big,
but my greatest fear when i see a stranger is that they will herald the arrival of heavy equipment
and one of those beautiful farms or forests will be eaten up by the cancerous growth of a new subdivision.
you can never be far enough out to feel completely safe.

my fears were soon allayed.
we were on the porch, getting ready to take big home to bigistan for the day, when we were startled by the cacaphonous racket of baying hounds. "they're out here hunting with dogs, big guy."
big was looking out into the woods, cocking his head from side to side.
he'd never heard anything like this.
then the shooting started.
big had heard something like that.
he's not afraid of thunder, or even fireworks.
but big knows just what a gunshot sounds like,
and he knows just what it can mean.

big came up to me and squeezed in between my feet.
then he looked up at me with his sad face,
before leaning against my leg and looking out into the woods.
it is a lot of responsibility to be able to fix anything.

the big year: winter and spring

while we couldn't see thru the woods,
we could tell the sounds were coming from either ben's farm or mr brothers place.
i knew ben and susan wouldn't have given anyone permission to hunt on their place with dogs, so while big tried to shrink even further into my lap, listening to the re-enactment of the battle of liberty gap with dogs
i called susan.

i didn't even get to ask...

"there are six carloads of people over on mr brothers' place, hunting with dogs."
what we couldn't figure out was what they were hunting.
nothing is in season right now.
we settled on coyotes,
because there is no season on coyotes.
but there aren't enough coyotes in the county to generate the fusillades that followed one after another.
were they shooting (hopefully) at nothing?
or were they shooting anything that moved?

i didn't have the heart to take big to bigistan,
and leave him cowering in fear in his bigloo.
but i couldn't sit on the porch indefinitely.
when i finally had to go inside,
big begged to come with me.
i had to tell him he'd have to settle for his bed behind the fireplace;
"you'll be safe there, big guy. it's gonna be alright."

it was after noon before the safari finally ended.
i reckon they had killed or driven off every living creature they could find. big was relieved to go to bigistan for some peaceful lying in the sun.

me and little took our walk down that way, to see what we could see. we couldn't see anything, except a lot of tire tracks going thru mr brothers' pasture gate.

i will be watching anxiously over the next few days.
the warrior and the princess, our mating pair of redtails.
the big valley crow murder.

the short hares.
the turkeys.
the deer.
even the buzzards.
which, if any, of our friends have survived?

the brothers were out of town today.
so they missed the show.
not that it won't come up when they get back.
we see plenty of hunters out here.
that also comes with living in the country.
but those people don't hardly qualify as hunters.
i hope they don't have an invitation to ever return.
we don't need terror in bigistan.

laz

02-24-13
crowmunication

naturally me and big decided to walk thru the battleground this morning,
choosing a route that would go thru it both out and back.

we saw ben down near the end of the driveway.
he was fixing to start a 21.833333... mile training run on the big trail. he has spent some good training time on the big trail,
and i have told him (based on what people have told me)
that he can expect to run faster at his goal race (fall creek falls)
than his times have been on the big trail.
he has been encouraged by that,
i hope it turns out to be accurate.

as soon as he spotted ben,
the big was at the end of his leash,
straining like a sled dog,
half dragging me behind.
he likes ben.
i told him to "STOP!"
and he stopped.
"SIT!"
and he sat politely.

i felt sort of smug.
(see how under control my dog is!)
then i told him "OK"
and big was instantly at the end of his leash,
straining like a sled dog
half dragging me behind.

i'm sure glad i didn't brag out loud.

ben speculated that the hunting caravan had been on a rabbit safari. that sounded reasonable enough.
some people do hunt rabbits with dogs,
and a check last night revealed that rabbit season still had a few days to run.

after we left ben, we soon went around the curve into the war
zone. the first thing we heard was the cawing of a crow, near last
year's nesting site.
i was glad to hear that,
because apparently crow season is also open.
i don't know of anyone who hunts crows.
mostly they get shot by "hunters" who are just out to kill
anything they can.

i told big;
"i know you can't hunt crows with dogs.
crows are smarter than dogs!"
mr big didn't have anything to say to that.
sometimes my mouth gets a step or two ahead of my brain...

"present company excepted, big guy."
i don't think the apology did much good.
once words come out of my mouth,
i have not yet found a way to put them back.

so me and big focused on trying to spot our big valley crows.
it wasn't easy because they were all scattered out across the
whole valley.
they were calling to each other, so we could try to count.
but they were moving around, so it was hard.
at one point i thought i had identified four.
but at another, i wasn't sure there weren't six.
and six is one too many.
"can a solo crow join an established murder?"
big didn't know, and neither did i.

to make it more confusing,
there were crows from other murders along the boundaries,
and they were doing the same thing.
crow calls were to be heard in every direction,
fading off into the distance.

by the time we got to millersburg,
me and big had it figured out.

the crows are establishing their territories for the summer.
so on our way back thru the big valley, it was a lot easier to pick

the big year: winter and spring

out the big valley crows.
not only that, we were able to map out their territory.

back when me and big started roaming,
the big valley murder had nine or ten members,
and was the dominant murder in big territory.
last year, when they had declined to three,
a lot of big valley territory was lost to adjacent murders.
open fields are the heart of a murder's territory,
because that is where they forage for food.
wooded land serves as boundaries, and almost no man's lands
(or is that no crow's land?)
the big valley crows had claimed all of ben's 200 acres;
mostly open fields.
as well as the eastern 100 acres or so of mr brothers property,
(which is all directly across the road from ben's)
as well as 100 or so acres of adjacent farms to the east of mr
brothers' place, all the way to the woods on the ridge of hills on
the south side of the valley.
their western boundary includes the woods on our property,
the northern border is the wooded property on ben's north side.
to the east, they own maybe another 80 acres or so of the cow
pasture across the road from ben's place.
the eastern pasture abuts another murder's property in open
pastureland,
so without a wooded boundary, that border will be contentious
all year.
likewise, the part of the western border on mr brothers' farm is
on open land.
their nesting site last year is in the woods along mine and ben's
boundary.
all indications are that it will be their chosen location again this
year.

the big valley murder used to own all of mr brothers' land,
extending their domain almost all the way to short creek.
the short creek crows now own about 200 acres of pastureland
and hayfields that once belonged to the big valley band.
adding that to the several hundred acres they own along
fosterville road, the short creek crows are now the most
powerful family of crows in big territory.

in all, big territory includes the exclusive properties of at least 6 murders of crows
(the big valley band, the short creek murder, the east broiles and west broiles gangs, the fosterville road mob, and the millersburg birds)
and undoubtedly parts of at least that many more.
border wars go on endlessly,
keeping me and big amused.

we noticed a different player in the territory stakeout.
we saw solo crows flying high overhead,
cutting a straight line over one territory after another,
and calling continuously in distinctive three-caw bursts.
the crows down below responded, altho they gave no indication of flying up to challenge.
nor did the overflyers show any signs of wanting to come down and settle in.
me and big speculated that those are crows who have reached maturity,
(which can be after as much as 5 years in their birth murder)
and are striking out on their own, searching for mates and new homes.
they are waiting for the right response before they come down.

since each murder is essentally a single breeding pair,
along with various offspring and other family members,
things have to change once the breeding pair meet their end due to age or accident.
it would not be normal in the animal world for siblings to replace the breeders.
me and big speculated how these transitions might occur.
does the resident murder disperse,
and all new crows take over,
or does one of the members claim a mate from among these solo travelers,
and the murder gradually transitions to offspring of the new breeding pair?
it would be tough for a brand new breeding pair to stake out and defend enough space to successfully raise any young.
at least not by theirselves.

the big year: winter and spring

the more we learn about crows,
the more questions we have.

finishing up our morning workout,
me and big sat on the back porch and waited to see ben run past
the back side of bigistan.

he had to be pretty well into his 20 by now,
and we wanted to see how he looked.

while we waited we talked about all the birds we had been
seeing, and their preparations for spring.
it isn't just the crows.

we hadn't seen the redtail hawks this morning,
but that is not unusual.
we know that their territory covers at least that of the the short
creek and big valley crows,
along with both broiles road murders.
we suspect that it includes the hills to our south,
and some of the farmland to the north of the west broiles road
bunch. we don't see the hawks every day, as they move about
their home range, spending a few days at a time in each location.

the mockingbird males, including the rare squeaky gate bird, are
claiming their tiny territories.
the menfolk from the cardinals and bluebirds have gotten new
paint jobs;
so bright they almost hurt your eyes.
all the year-round birds are preparing for the upcoming spring.
these are exciting times.

and the migratory birds have already been in evidence.
earlier this week, we heard the warbling cries,
and looked up to see a large flock of sand hill cranes passing
overhead
(the second sighting in as many years, after never having seen
them before)
a pair of canada geese passed over and stopped briefly in ben's
hayfield as we were passing by.
they might be fooled by all the water that is around right now,
due to the rainy winter.
if so, they will be disappointed this summer, when it all dries up.

shoot, it isn't even going to be that long before the hummingbirds return from their vacations in central and south america.

things are hopping in me and big's territory.

and people ask; "what do you think about when you run?"
they ask it as if running is boring.
i think the real question should be;
"how do you absorb it all in that short of a time?"

laz

02-28-13
the purple dress

i read with amazement the discussion of books on tape,
to listen to while running.
and i wonder how come people cannot watch,
and listen to,
the real stories that unfold around them every day.

i saw the same show on crows as john (not the shepherd)
and, as it turned out, that helped me spot our local redtail hawk
pair the very next day.

the crows are all continuing their vigorous efforts in staking out territory
so the sounds of crows cawing are ubiquitous.
however, big and i had barely gotten started on our daily rounds
when a different tone to a crow caw caught my ear.
i recognized the alarm call that i had heard on nova the previous night.

as big and i walked, i searched in the direction of the call until i spotted the bird.
changing my focus to the direction of his attention,
it only took a few seconds to spot the familiar shape of a hawk perched on a limb.
then i began looking for the mate.
lately the pair have been almost inseparable...
like any young lovers.
and i could see that the crow, soon joined by a team-mate,
was giving the hawk a wider berth than normal.
the crows are always more cautious around both hawks.

sure enough, i soon spotted the mate.
i was relieved that they, like our big valley crows, had survived the slaughter.

me and big continued, making our broiles road loop.
with a little luck we could get a reading on the status of some
more of the murders that live in our running territory.
we have figured out a pattern to this time of territorial claimstaking.

each murder will disperse individually to the boundaries,
where they call out to neighboring crows
and move about.
it is remarkably difficult to pin down how many crows are in
each group.

however, they periodically regroup in a central location,
and walk about on the ground talking among themselves,
while one member stands guard in a tree.
when we find a murder gathered in war council we can count
them.
me and big wonder what the crows are saying.
are they plotting strategy?
are they discussing ground lost and gained?
only the crows know.

the big valley group is facing varying pressure on different
borders.
as we walk thru the center of their territory we can hear that
they are getting a lot of pressure from the south.
i had thought the hundreds of acres of wooded hills would have
been a good buffer zone,
but maybe the band on their south has grown.
maybe they covet the good open pasturelands of the brothers
place.
maybe they are getting pressure from their own neighbors.

the north and east borders seem secure.
we don't know much about the neighbors on the east,
but a half hour later we are on the north side of the wooded
boundary,
traveling west, thru the heart of the east broiles murder,
the northern neighbor,
and we find them gathered in council in a hayfield.
they are down to five members,
no wonder they aren't pushing in from the north.

as we approach the boundary of the east and west broiles
murders,
we see one of the large migrating nomadic bands of crows flying
south.
the large flocks of crows don't travel like most flocks of birds,

the big year: winter and spring

moving simultaneously, wheeling and turning in synchronization.
they remind me more of human runners on a group run,
all moving individually, some forging ahead, others straggling behind the main body.

the leaders cross the road well ahead of us, and come down to land in the top of a huge oak tree in no crow's land.
as we approach, we can see all the following crows
drop down in turn, and join the group.
by the time we are passing the tree, the last stragglers have come in.
i lost count as the biggest group landed,
but there are more than 20 crows all cawing and talking and hopping around in the crown of the tree.
they had probably been strung out over more than a mile,
but are now all together,
like a group of runners taking a break.

then a few birds take off and continue to the south.
the others follow in ones and twos, and even a large bunch in the middle.
the road curves to the south just past the tree,
and we can see the last crows taking off.
just like the human runner counterparts, the stragglers get the least rest.

me and big discuss these nomadic groups,
so different from the permanent murders that live here.
are they traveling to some distant location?
if so, why would they be going so determinedly south in the spring?
are they pre-breeding age,
or do they have a mass nesting site somewhere around?
is there just not enough land for them to live in their own family groups?
or are they part of a whole different crow culture?
i know we see them all year round,
sometimes stopping to forage in an established murder's territory for a day or two
before moving on.
and the outnumbered local murders do not challenge them.

nor do they interact in any way.
they simply keep their distance until the nomadic band moves
on, even tho the nomads might occupy favorite foraging grounds.

so much about crows that we do not know.
it isn't anything like an audio book.
no narrator to clear things up in a few miles.
all we can do is continue to observe and try to figure it out.
probably we will never know all the answers.

we pass thru the west broiles crows' territory and hear them
working their borders,
as we approach the goat corner,
we are surprised to find the goat corner dog's house is gone.
it is almost too much to hope that she might be gone.
at least for today we don't have to deal with her,
as she makes no appearance.

the goat corner marks the western edge of west broiles territory,
and there we we find another mystery.
we see another large murder on the other side of the cow
pasture.
i can count thirteen crows, again gathered in the top of a massive
tree.
but this group is not taking a rest.
as we watch, small groups of three to five birds fly off in different
directions,
returning to rejoin the main group after a few minutes.
we can't see where they are going,
or what they are doing,
because they are going into the fields beyond the treeline
marking the west broiles boundary.

thirteen would be the biggest local murder i ever saw.
almost an impossible number for one family.
but it would be the smallest nomadic band i have seen.
is it the murder from that border,
about which me and big know nothing,
or is it a new murder of crows,
trying to squeeze out a permanent territory between existing
murders?

maybe the murder on that side has winked out of existence,
and they are claiming unowned territory?

"we could use a narrator, mr big. the more we figure out, the less we know."
big says nothing, but i am sure he agrees.

we have a few uneventful miles to ponder all these mysteries,
except for running into the goat corner dog.
at least one mystery is solved,
altho why her house has been removed is still unknown.
then we come on the short creek murder having a council on the old miller place.
they are down to four members this year,
and over the past few days we have watched the big valley murder push them back on their western border,
reclaiming about 50 acres of cow pasture that the short creek bunch took last spring,
when the big valley murder was hovering on the edge with only three members.
no mystery there.
the short creek crows are down this year,
and they are being pressed on the other side by the fosterville road gang.

by this time we were less than a mile from home.
but the mysteries were not quite over.

the pug house has become a real nuisance to pass.
wondering if today will be the day the insane pit bull's chain gives, and staving off the attempts of the always loose aussie to bite our heels.
she hasn't succeeded in biting me or amy yet,
but she got ben the other day.
the replacement pug hasn't yet acquired the disposition of his predecessor,
but he is getting there.
and now they have added a new dog to the mix...

a chihuahua.

me and big always try to approach quietly,
hoping to pass unnoticed.

that doesn't happen often,
with so many eyes watching.
and today is not going to be the exception.
the pug house dogs spot us way down the road,
and they are all out in the road waiting for us
(except the insane pit bull, who is just lunging at the end of his chain)
big's hackles are up.
he hates the pughouse dogs as much as i do,
and he has to really work to stay on task while i stave them off with the threat of my trainer.

as we get closer, i can see that the chihuahua has been outfitted in some sort of sweater...

then i start laughing.
it is no sweater;
that poor dog is wearing the ugliest purple dress that has ever been inflicted on a dog.
even as she yaps and runs at our heels,
i am sure i can see the shame in her eyes.
"this one, big; this is a mystery i will never figure out."

i mean, who the heck thinks spagetti straps look good on a chihuahua?

laz

03-05-13
coyote hunters don't help

there are a lot of challenges for a big during a daily walk.
maintaining discipline doesn't come easy,
for a dog who is set on high all the time.

and coyote hunters don't help.

the coyotes are elusive,
but me and big know where the coyote hunters are.

one morning just after sunrise,
we were walking along past the winston place
when we heard what sounded sort of like a coyote howling.
the timing was all wrong.
coyotes don't howl after sunup.
and the sound wasn't quite right.
none the less, big was very interested in what was going on.

then i spotted the coyote hunters' pickup parked down the road.

another morning we heard a sort of bleating call.
maybe it was supposed to sound like an animal in distress.
this time i knew to look for the coyote hunters' truck.

i wasn't sure how many coyotes they were fooling,
but they were driving big nuts.

then the dead coyotes started showing up.

we found the first one in the ditch beside the road to fosterville hill. a week later we found one beside the road to millersburg. over the past couple of months we have found four different dead coyotes; all alongside the roads leading to and from our little valley.

 me and big don't know if the coyote hunters are simply lazy in disposing of their kill or if the corpses are supposed to be a warning to the coyotes.
the one thing they do accomplish,

is making it hard for the big to stay on task.
he wants desperately to go and inspect the bodies.

mr winston is pretty pleased with the work of the coyote
hunters, but i have my reservations.
every one of the dead coyotes so far have been pups.
they don't even have their permanent teeth fully grown in.

and we can still hear the coyotes howling at night.

i'm not sure what problems the coyotes are supposed to be
causing. but i am sure that the coyote hunters don't help.

and big wants to be a good dog every day.
i know for sure the coyote hunters don't help that.

laz

03-09-13
the talking dog

so now he has sandra doing it.

she has complained at me because;
"you talk to that dog like he is a person."

i would quit if he didn't seem to understand.

but what really got to her is when i started a sentence with;
"big said..."

"now how did he say that?" she would snap back
"does he talk to you?"

"well, not exactly. but he gets his point across."

so last weekend i had to be gone a couple of days to do some barkley work. i got lucky, because big's team-member, dale, was willing to come and take big for his walk on one of those days.
so, that night i called home,
and i asked how big did on his walk...

"it went pretty well. when they got back dale fed him, and he ate...he told dale that he was supposed to stay on the porch, but dale took him back to bigistan anyway."

i didn't ask her;
"now how did big tell him that? did he talk?"

later i saw dale, and he reported on the big's performance.
apparently big did better than he does for me.
he never pulled or tried to take a side-trip into the bushes.
just like a kid, they act better around other people than they do around their own family...

of course, also like a kid, he took advantage.
he seems to have sent out a lot more pee-mails than i usually allow.
and;
"he tried to convince me he was supposed to stay on the porch.

but i wasn't so sure about that.
i put him on his cable anyway."

"and i saw his food dish was full, so i fed him."
that is big.
he has his own ideas about how things should be,
and he thinks he should work for his food.
i used to think he wouldn't eat because i was gone.
he just doesn't eat if he doesn't do his job.

i took big to the bank the other day.
i went without him once, and now i know better.
as soon as i came in the door, i was met with;
"where's big?"

i have to remember who is the star in this family.

so i took big with me this week, and the teller took a daring step.
they usually give me a dog biscuit to give big.
i can understand their reluctance to put their hand in front of
that enormous mouth....with all those huge teeth.
they are usually amazed at how delicately he takes the treat from
my palm. this day, one of the ladies got daring.
she gave big a treat.

he took it, then he hopped his front feet down off the counter,
walked over to me and laid it at my feet. then he looked up at me.
"what is it big? did you not do your work?"

i picked up the biscuit and he immediately SAT and licked his
lips. i held it in front of his nose and told him to "WAIT!"
he licked his lips again and stared eagerly at the treat.

after making him sit and wait for an ample enough time i told
him "OK!" and he deftly removed the treat from my palm and
crunched it up with wagging tail.

the bank ladies found that fascinating, so i explained;
"he feels like he needs to work for his food."

they did not ask me;
"how did he tell you that? does he talk?"

laz

03-12-13
the sensitive guy

i fell down on my job this morning.

i was letting big get in a little post-run sunning on the back porch when the fedex guy came.
i usually already have taken him to spend the day in bigistan, but he had staked out a cozy spot on the porch and was snoring loudly, so i left him snoozing while i went inside to call about some rock.

pre-occupied, i didn't notice him leave until sophie and little started barking.
big was no longer on the porch, and we had company...

uh-oh!!

i saw the back end of the fedex truck as i came off the porch, and then big came running around the corner to meet me.
he had on his big happy face,
and the fed-ex man was following him.

"sorry, i try to get out and greet visitors before big does."
the fedex guy just laughed;
"when i saw him come around the corner of the house, i thought i was in trouble. but then i saw his tail wagging."

big trotted back out to the fedex guy,
and made himself available to pet.
the fedex man reached down and scratched the top of big's head, big closed his eyes with pleasure and wagged his tail harder.
i can see why sandra is worried about what that dog might do.
if they start training cats to deliver packages,
no good will come of it.
as long as people do it,
big thinks they all love him...

or they will, once he introduces himself.

but that is because big is a sensitive guy.
he reads people about as well as he does dogs.

(i wish i had his gift)
the only problem is that he always feels personally responsible.
if people are afraid of him, he is afraid of them.
if they are happy, he is happy.
and if they are out of sorts, big thinks it is his fault.

one day i was working on something on the back porch.
big was there being my assistant;
assisting by watching everything i did with great interest.
it wasn't coming out to suit me, and i kept getting more and more frustrated.
finally, i let out a string of curses.
it helped me let off some steam,
but i saw big's back end disappearing around the corner of the house.
when i went and looked,
he was peering out at me from the bigloo, looking worried.
you have to be careful around sensitive guys.

after the girl's state finals the other night, i got home late.
sophie and little were in the pen,
wound up tight because supper was late.
big had, naturally, taken off his cable after it got dark,
and he was waiting on the porch.
as you would expect with the big,
he wasn't concerned about supper.
he was just glad to see me get home.

now bringing sophie and little in to eat is a trick.
we should have named them mayhem and chaos...

and that is when supper is on time.

i bring them in one at a time.
sandra made fun of me until the first time she had to bring them in. together they aren't mayhem plus chaos....
they are mayhem times chaos.

so i went to the pen, and commanded mayhem and chaos to "SIT!" and "WAIT!"
knowing there would be no supper until they followed orders,
the short bus dogs sat, their tails sweeping the stone floor of their cage furiously.

the big year: winter and spring

then came my real trick....
"LITTLE... OK!"
little tore out of the pen like a tornado,
and shot off into the woods.
sophie stayed put.

i feel pretty smug about my trick,
because when sandra opens the pen, both dogs shoot out at once,
and almost bowl her over.
there is no "SITTING" and "WAITING."

i saw big coming down the steps,
the sight of little racing around the woods aroused his play
instinct...

"stay on the porch big, we don't need your help."
actually, what i didn't need was little rolled in the dirt and leaves
before i took her inside,
not to mention how much longer the process would take.
little is most efficient when she winds herself down.
I wasn't of a mind to take longer than necessary.
my supper was late, too.
and i couldn't even start cooking until i took care of the animals.

little was nothing but a white streak, tearing thru the dark
woods. i wonder at her ability to do this without crashing into
something during the day,
much less after dark.
she must know where every tree and vine is located.

after a few minutes, little came flying up the steps,
puffing like a steam engine.
now; i had told big to stay on the porch...

and he did.

i didn't think to tell him not to play.
he met little at my legs,
and a spontaneous game of chase each other around the maypole
(my legs) broke out.
sophie started barking, lest i forget that she was next.
i tried to steer little towards the door, i tried to steer big out of
the way.

then hunger got the best of me, and i got short;
"BIG! WHY DON'T YOU GO LAY IN YOUR BED AND GET OUT OF THE WAY!!"
big trotted off quickly in the direction i was pointing, and lay down on his bed watching me.

i got little inside, waiting at her feeding spot,
then i got sophie.
sophie was a bit more trouble,
because if big is on the porch she wants to run to him, roll over on her back, and pee on herself.
it was less trouble than usual, because big never budged.

i got mayhem and chaos fed, then i brought big his food.
he had not moved a millimeter,
and lay there on his bed, watching me with those big, soulful eyes.
i showed him his food bowl.
he didn't move.
i shook it, so the pebbles of food would rattle.
he didn't move.
"you're all right big guy. you aren't in trouble. you can come out and eat."
big cautiously came out, crossed the porch, and "SAT!".
when i gave him the "OK!" to eat,
he spent extra time with his head buried in my lap, getting petted.
i had to tell him to "go on and eat, big fella" several times before he could tear himself away...

and people find it necessary to beat these dogs?

but it was last night that big showed the depth of his sensitivity.
me and big were on the back porch having some us time when amy got home from work.
he was sitting between my feet, leaned up against my leg, with his head on my knee, while i petted him.
when amy got there she was as wound up as a little over something that happened at work.
she didn't even stop to pet the big before she started unloading.
i knew it was bad, because she was telling me about it.
i am not the best sympathetic ear around....

the big year: winter and spring

big is.

when amy started talking, big's head slipped off my knee.
as she went on, his head just kept drooping lower, and lower, and lower.
finally she took a breath, and i told her;
"you are breaking big's heart."
she looked down at the big, he was absolutely dejected,
his nose was almost touching the ground.
amy leaned down to scratch under his chin;
"i'm sorry big, it isn't your fault!"
she coaxed him into raising up, until he put his head back on my knee.
from there he watched with his best sad-eyed expression while she told the rest of her story...

being certain to periodically stroke his huge head to reassure the big that everything was ok.
and it wasn't his fault.

i understand that women love sensitive guys.
no wonder big is such a ladies' man.

laz

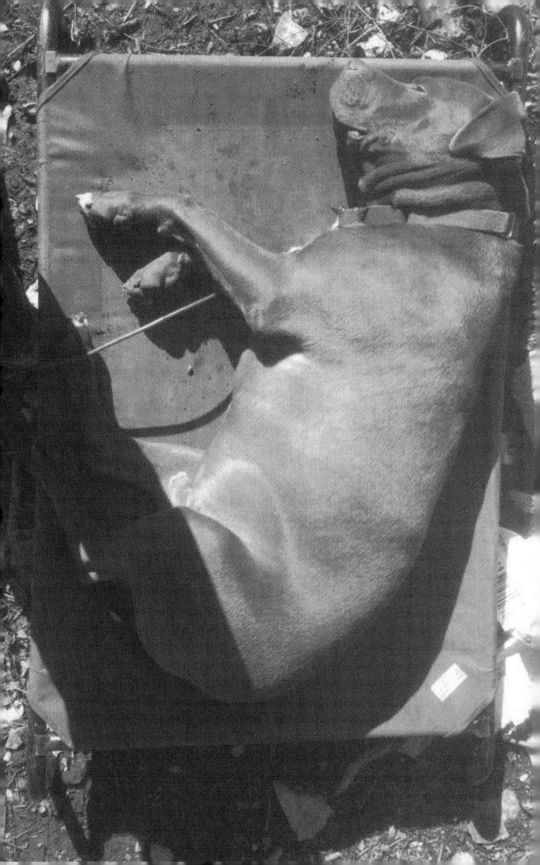

03-17-13
a big future

me and big got an early start yesterday.
i had to leave for frozen head to do some barkley work,
so the big was already out on his cable when the first rays of sunshine filtered thru the trees.

the day's work was completed a little early,
so we took the opportunity to hike a short trail at frozen head,
one i had never done in all these years, because i am always going somewhere further and don't have time.

it had turned into the first really nice day of spring,
and the trail, which was short and gentle, and led to a couple of small waterfalls,
had beckoned many a local off their couches and out from in front of their televisions.

since the way out was on a gentle uphill grade,
most of the other hikers were leaving me and my bad leg behind.
one family group, however,
i noticed we were catching.
when we got close enough, the reason was obvious.
they had a small puppy on a leash,
and everyone who passed them on the return trip
was stopping to pet the little dog.
people love puppies,
which works out well,
since puppies love people.
as we gradually closed on the puppy people,
i could see a familiar look about it.

the puppy people got to the waterfall just a few minutes ahead of us, and the teenage boy who had been walking the dog handed the leash to his mother
and went over to climb on the rocks around the waterfall.

i went over to where she was standing,
holding the leash while the puppy tried to run this way and that.
the animal was a very pretty white and blue-gray,
with a shiny coat.

a very familiar face looked up at me.
the broad anvil of a head,
floppy little batwing ears,
wide set almond eyes,
the irises blue and milky white...

giving it a look that was unique as a puppy.
but someday will be described as the frightening stare of a
soulless killer.

i asked if i could pet the puppy,
altho i would only be the 100th person to do it that day.
then i sat on a rock.
the puppy promptly climbed into my lap,
and then leaned back against me,
a move so familiar, big might have given her lessons.
those arresting eyes stared up into mine.

"what kind of a dog is she?"
"we don't know. my son rescued her."
"i know what kind of a dog this is. you have a baby pit bull."

the lady did not look very happy to hear that.
she was quiet for a little while.
the puppy, having stared as long as was polite,
laid her head on my arm and looked out at the people around the
waterfall, while my hands roamed about hitting the sweet spots.
no trick to that on a baby big.
bigs are one endless sweet spot.
finally she said;
"the vet said maybe 65%... my son rescued her."

i wondered where he came up with 65%,
of all the strange numbers.
"don't listen to all the stories. these are wonderful dogs."

i asked her if they had started training her.
yes, they were working on it.
but it was her son's dog.
"you'll want to work with her. but these are very intelligent dogs.
she will want to please him.
but you should stay with it,

the big year: winter and spring

because she will be very strong later on."
"she is amazingly strong right now."

we talked a few minutes more.
she was not overjoyed that her son had rescued a pit.
i can understand how she feels. we hear so much.
i assured her that "these dog's love people."
and that they do.
some breeds love to hunt, some to herd.
some are natural guard dogs, others beasts of burden.
given any chance at all pit bulls love people.
some of them don't get that chance...

and love people anyway.

as i left, i looked back at the lady and the puppy.
more people had stopped to pet her.
everyone loves puppys.
and i thought about the little dog's future.

6 months from now, the public reception would be very different.
once she was big enough that everyone knew what she was...

the same people would recoil in horror when they saw her
coming. even now, the tennessee legislature is considering a bill
to declare all pit bulls "vicious dogs."
i hoped against hope that teenage boy would not lose interest in
his project.
if he does what he needs to do, he will have a dog like no other.

if he fails, it is the dog who will pay.
i thought about my big fella back home.
probably already back up on the porch,
waiting for me to come home.

i hope that puppy has a big future.
in it's innocence, it thinks everyone loves it.
it has no idea that people can be mean.
but it has been born into a hostile world.

laz

03-23-13
the big stink

it was a typical friday night.
i was dogsitting sophie for amy
the sophe and the little mostly occupying themselves
and big was out on the porch in his usual spot.

around 2000 hours, sophie and little indicated they needed to go outside.
they do this by standing at the door and staring intently out.

i have learned better than to let sophie and little go out together.
individually they are pretty obedient.
together, they tend to get caught up in the excitement of the moment and it takes a while to get them back.

i almost let them go out together.
it was raining, and they are usually more than willing to come back in when it rains.
generally it takes some urging to get them to go on out at all.
dogs have no sense of time, and no grasp of the concept of inevitable.
if the weather isn't right, they figure they can just wait till later, indefinitely.

i had to do some urging with the little.
"go DO IT, little."
"GO ON! GO DO IT!"
little's look clearly said;
"that's alright. it is too wet. i just won't pee tonight."
"LITTLE. GO DO IT. you have to pee eventually, you goober."
little made her excursion without incident,
going out into the edge of the woods to do her business,
and then returning.
then it was sophie's turn.

sophie had ideas of her own,
tonight she was not concerned about the rain.
when i opened the door and gave her the ok she was off like a shot, down the steps, and vanished into the woods.

black dogs disappear in the night.

within seconds the sounds of her crashing thru the brush faded
away, leaving nothing but my voice echoing in the night.
"SOPHIE, COME ON SOPHIE!"

after a while i gave up and came back in the house grumbling.
looks like we are back to going out on a leash....
dumb dog.

i checked the porch periodically.
amy would be crushed if something happened to her dog.
i called.
but there was no use.
sophie would be back when she darn well felt like it.
big just raised up his head and watched.

little was more worried than i was.
she alternately watched out the door,
and came over and made her strange honking noise at me.
sophie is supposed to be inside at night.
sleeping with her head resting on the little.

three hours later, little told me sophie was back.
sure enough, i looked out the door and there was sophie looking
back at me....

wagging her tail like nothing had happened.

"i can tell time, sophie."
she just grinned at me. not a sign of guilt.
i opened the door and went out to dry her off...

and found out sophie had not come back alone.
she had perfumed herself up thoroughly with her favorite scent;
eau de rotting flesh.
i was reminded of one of the great mysteries of the dog world:
i can take a piece of meat the size of a pinhead, seal it in a jar,
place the jar inside 3 ziplock baggies,
and steam clean the whole package...

when i step on the back porch, big can smell it from his bigloo.

the big year: winter and spring

yet when we are walking, and he comes on a strange poop
(that i can smell from 50 feet away)
he puts his nose about a millimeter from it, and sniffs like crazy.

and he is mystified that i don't let him roll in rotting roadkill.

all musing aside,
i needed to decide what to do with sophie.
what do you do with a wet dog that smells like a week-old, sun-ripened corpse?
at midnight?

the bad voice said;
"stick her in amy's room and close the door."

the good voice said;
"scrub her clean and dry her off,
so amy won't come home to a stinky dog."

the reasonable voice said;
"just leave her butt on the porch for amy to worry about."

i left her there about 10 minutes, before i peeked out the door to see what the sophster was doing.

she was gone again.

i went out and discovered that this time big had gone with her.
(i have to warn my big boy about running with the wrong crowd)

at least this time i didn't have to worry about one dog coming back. i called a couple of times, and whistled.
then i waited.
in just a few minutes big came at a dead run,
tail wagging, looking like his usual happy self.
"you know you aren't supposed to go off at night."
big hung his head.
"you'll have to stay out at the bigloo if you don't behave."
big double timed it to his bed, and lay there looking at me.
big, for all his fearsome appearance, is terribly sensitive.

about that time, sophe came trailing up the steps.
"and you can wait in the pen until amy gets home."

the big dog diaries

after i put sophie in the pen,
i had to stop on the way in and reassure my big guy;
i leaned down and gave him a scratch behind his ears
(among his thousand favorite pettings)
"you're a good dog, that comes when he is called."
big wagged his tail.
all was well in the big world again.

laz

03-24-13
sweetie

perhaps she was an angel.

sweetie turned up about the time janet first got sick.
she didn't know it at the time,
but deep inside janet, renegade cells were busy multiplying...
invading...
spreading thru her body.

one day janet went out to the garage to go to the store.
at the door she was stopped short.
in the back of the garage the face of a demon stared back at her.
a pair of big black eyes glittered in the half-light,
set in a wide face on an enormous head.
a huge, grinning mouth split the massive head.
knots of muscle outlined a massive chest and shoulders,
and a washboard of ribs gave silent testimony to a starving animal.

no one who meets a strange pit-bull unexpectedly
will soon forget the experience.

back in the house, it was not the image of those gaping jaws that filled janet's mind.
it was the protruding ribs.
anyone who knew janet would first tell you that she was kind to animals.
living on a farm, where society's discarded rejects show up all too often,
janet could never turn her back on a hungry, injured or homeless creature.
this was who she was.

soon she was back at the garage,
this time bearing food and water.
the starving dog accepted the offerings gratefully,
but when janet started back to the house,
sweetie abandoned the nourishment, and followed janet.
it was the beginning of a love story.

of course, sweetie loved everybody.
strangers were greeted like long lost friends,
and family members like royalty.
grandchildren and great grandchildren could poke and prod,
and ride her like a horse.
sweetie stood in stoic acceptance.
these were her family, and it was her job to please them.

sweetie loved everyone,
but from that first day, she was janet's dog.
if janet made an appearance, all others were abandoned and
forgotten.

and sweetie was good for janet.
heredity had played a cruel trick on janet,
her dna bringing the gift of a degenerative bone disorder.
her bones were brittle and fragile. breaks were frequent.
her vertebrae were crumbling.
for janet, life meant choosing between living in a drug induced
fog or enduring pain.

maybe dogs are such great comfort to the suffering
precisely because they cannot speak.
we humans want so bad to have an answer.
to uncover some cure, to proffer up some wisdom that will make
everything better.
sometimes there is nothing that can be done.
sometimes all that is needed is silent company.
dogs are good at that.
sweetie was the best.

and so life went on at barry and janet's place.
not, perhaps, perfect.
but good.
and sweetie was an integral part of that goodness.
part clown, part protector, part friend, and part confidante.
like most pit bulls,
her intelligence and good disposition made it impossible not to
smile when she was around.
and she was always around.

then one day janet found out about the cancer.
it had silently gone about its work,

the big year: winter and spring

spreading out to the furthest reaches of her body.
maybe if it weren't for the pain she already endured,
janet might have noticed it sooner.
maybe that would have made a difference.

maybe and perhaps.
small words on which so much hinges.

there was no question that janet would fight.
who would her children call in times of stress?
who would dote on the grandchildren and great grandchildren?
who would care for the abandoned and helpless animals?

it was not a battle.
it was a war.
it was a war where victories were few and fleeting.
janet was assaulted with an array of powerful drugs,
that wracked and tortured her body.
sometimes the cancer would briefly lose some ground,
but always it gathered itself, and came back with a vengeance.

life goes on, and people have to work to survive...
even when they have more pressing issues on their mind.
janet spent many days alone...
except for sweetie.
sweetie, who could offer comfort the way only a loyal dog can do.
sweetie was there in times of loneliness and despair.
sweetie was there to see janet off to the hospital,
and to greet her when she came home.

near the end, janet was not able to go outside very much.
but sweetie was always waiting.
the sound of janet's voice would bring sweetie at a run,
from wherever she was,
to wait at the door...

just in case.

there finally came a day when there were no more treatments to
try, no matter how powerful, no matter how experimental.
janet was reduced to a shell of her former self,
and slept most of the time.
there came that day when she told barry;

"i just don't think i can fight any more."
barry told her that it was all right. that he understood.

the next morning, about 0500 hours,
janet died peacefully in her sleep.

all day long, the people came.
family and friends gathering, as people are wont to do
at times like this.
sweetie was there to greet each of them.
barry and i spent a long time sitting on the porch
(away from the throngs inside the house)
with sweetie sitting between us getting petted.
i wanted to have the answer that would make everything better.
but i have learned a little something from the dogs.
i just mostly listened.
i'm not as good at it as sweetie.
but i did my best.

the next morning sweetie was gone.

barry looked for her for weeks.
he drove endless miles around the county,
looking and calling.
he hung up flyers everywhere people might stop.
but no trace of sweetie was ever found.

barry told me he thought maybe she had gone to look for janet...

maybe.

or perhaps she was an angel.

laz

04-02-13
the big organizational chart

big may have to come to the barkley next year.
it seems that he has revised the organizational chart...

laz is still in that top box
(obviously big has not consulted sandra on this)
and in the next box, right underneath,
is laz' executive assistant; the big.

with me gone, big simply did not stay on his cable.
he preferred the back porch.
sandra returned him to bigistan.
amy returned him to bigistan.
he practically followed them back to the porch.

they tried telling him what to do.
he just gave them that big, goofy grin;
"i am only a dumb old dog.
i don't know what you want me to do?"

his friends dale and linda came and took him for walks a couple of times.
they found him waiting on the porch.

the first time, big kind of dragged his feet.
he might have thought i was going to show up for his walk.
he does the same thing if amy tries to take him running before we take our walk.
after all, he is my assistant.
it is his job to go everywhere with me.
if he is off running,
i might go walking without him.

dale finally stopped and asked;
"what is it you want to do, big?"

big turned around and faced back towards the house.

he picks his times to be a "dumb old dog."

the big dog diaries

the next time was a different story.
dale said;
"when we got back to the driveway, big didn't want to turn in.
he wanted to keep going"

after convincing the big that it was time to go home,
they took him and put him back on his cable,
before starting for home.

dale and linda had reached the pug house,
where the dog menagerie always barks at them
(just like they do everyone)
as usual the aussie was trying to sneak around to get in a bite
from behind,
when suddenly he took off.

dale and linda looked around to see big coming down the road
like a runaway locomotive.
his face was alight with joy,
his tongue flapping out the side of his mouth.
"i knew you weren't finished. good thing i know how to take off
my cable!"

and so it was that sandra was not happy with big when i got
home.
"he just thinks he can do as he pleases."
amy was not happy with big, either.
usually when she lets sophie out for her morning business
big is gone with me already.

if he is on the porch when either of the short bus dogs goes out,
i have to be ready to remind him;
"big! they do not need your help to pee!"

so amy cornered me when i got home.
"sophie has not gotten to pee in peace in 4 days...

she has to pee with big dive-bombing her."
i had to stifle a grin and look serious.
i know how much big likes to jump over sophie
(a game that sophie finds flat out terrifying)
i could see his face in my minds eye,

the big year: winter and spring

that big silly grin, his eyes twinkling with laughter.
why can't a dog have a sense of humor?

looking at amy's face, i could see she had no sense of humor.
i thought better of pointing out that big was just being helpful.
when he jumps over sophie, the pee comes out.

then she told me;
"and if she wanted to poop, she had to do it on the run..."

that did it.
i had to go outside for a smoke...

so she wouldn't see me laughing.
big was waiting for me.
"big, you're going to have to let sophie and little do their business without your help.
because you are no help at all."

i couldn't tell if big was paying attention or not.
he was too busy trying to touch as much of me as possible.

because, despite apparently living without rules,
big might have been the most unhappy of all.
when i got home at 0200 hours,
he greeted me with quiet desperation.
tired as i was,
we spent about an hour just sitting on the porch with his head in my lap.

the next day,
while i unloaded a van-load of barkley stuff into the garage,
big walked back and forth with me,
in perfect heel formation.
he didn't care if we walked the same 20 feet a hundred times.
we had some together to make up.

i'm not sure how he knew,
but when i got the last of the stuff to go in the house,
big hopped in the van, and sat right in the middle grinning at me.

i asked him to come out.
but big was suddenly stricken with the "dumb dog disorder"
and just continued to grin at me.

111

the big dog diaries

i leaned in to get him by the collar,
and he moved to the very back...

and sat there grinning at me.

i went around and opened the back door.
big decided he would be happier in the passenger seat.

i opened the passenger door
and he hopped over into the driver's seat.

so i had to put my foot down.
"ok big guy. fun and games are over. you have to get out."

his grin vanished.
his head hung.
he wearily (and oh so slowly) climbed out of the van.
that's how we went back to bigistan.
me leading, big following.
his nose almost dragging the ground,
with the weight of the world on his shoulders.

"you have to stay here while i turn in the van, big guy."

when i stopped at the little house
to put the rest of the stuff into storage,
i could hear big barking for me to come back for him.

sure enough, as i came out for the second load,
there was big, turning the corner at the bottom of the hill.
his happy face was back;
"you accidentally left me on my cable...

good thing i know how to take it off!"
he accompanied me while i offloaded the last of the stuff,
then he went and stood next to the passenger door.

have i ever mentioned that big is strong-willed?

"big. you have to go back. you can't go with me."
his head dropped, and he took one step towards me.

then he stopped and looked up hopefully.

the big year: winter and spring

"big. you have to go back to bigistan."

one more step.

"big. i have to return the van today."

then something caught his attention,
and he looked out at the road.
a moment later, three bicycles went clicking past.

big watched them until they went out of sight,
then he turned and hightailed it for bigistan.
he didn't even glance my way as he went past.

when i got to bigistan,
he was waiting patiently by his cable.

big is no fool.
there has never been a bicycle in bigistan.

i have until the vol-state to think of a different plan for the big.
or maybe i can just hire a bicyclist to ride back and forth past the house.

laz

04-07-13
big greetings

big knows his cars.
big knows all kinds of things.

when the newspaper lady is coming he starts wagging his tail.
she always stops and pets him.

she was sick for about 3 months,
and someone else ran the route for her.
they drove the same car,
but big paid no attention to them.
i didn't realize it wasn't her until the car drove right past.
apparently he can not only recognize car motors,
he can tell who is driving.

her first day back she was driving a different car.
big started wagging his tail and turned around to watch her drive up. this time she didn't just stop and pet him out the window.
she got out and gave him a hug.
i'm not gonna guess how big got that one.

big knows when i come home in my car.
if he is on the porch, he runs out to greet me.
if he is in bigistan,
he barks for me to come and get him.

when amy comes home in her car.
if big is on the porch, he runs out to greet her.
if he is in bigistan,
he just continues with whatever he is doing.

when sandra comes home in her car.
if big is on the porch, he shrinks back further into his cubbyhole.
if he is in bigistan,
he lays low in his bigloo...

big is no fool.

when i come home in my truck,
big comes running around to watch the garage door open.
he is fascinated by it.

this afternoon i came home in my truck.
big came tearing around the house
(i was late. if i'm not there by suppertime, he takes off his cable.)
and stood transfixed while the garage door opened.
after i pulled in, i looked back.

big had come up and was sitting almost directly under the garage
door, and was sitting there looking up at it intently.
he knew it would close in just a few seconds.
i hollered at the big;
"hey big guy; what's so fascinating about the garage door?"
big wagged his tail, but he didn't take his eyes off the door.
"silly goober."
that was worth another quick wag.

while the door closed,
big came inside and looked up where it was coming out real
hard, altho he moved out of the way before the door got so low
he triggered the kickback.
the door gobbled up my view of the big,
kind of like the cheshire cat,
except instead of that big grin,
the last thing to disappear was his feet.

and then it dawned on me.
i know why he is so mesmerized by the garage door.
he doesn't know how to open it!
it's the only darn thing on the farm he can't open.

makes me feel a lot better.
maybe he can identify cars by sound before i can even hear them.
maybe he knows who is driving before he can even see them.
but he don't know nothin' about radio controls.
we humans still have our secrets...

i just need to figure out how, when big is with me,
to open and close the door without him seeing how i do it.

laz

spring 2013

hello.
my name is big
and i love the spring.

in the spring my master takes me for long walks.
in the spring there are big storms
and master comes to sit on the porch
and we watch the rain together.

in the spring there are lots of birds
and rabbits and squirrels
all running and playing.

in the spring the streams fill with water,
and master stops
to let me wade and splash in the water.

the summer is the perfect time of year.

in the spring the lizards run across the porch
and squirrels chase each other thru the trees.
tiny birds try to steal my food
so i can chase them away
and the grass grows tall and soft
for me to roll around and snap at the air.

in the spring the trails grow shady and cool
and i can hide in the weeds.

spring feels so good.

i love the spring.
i wish it lasted all year.

big

04-08-13
the big incident

no matter how hard you try,
it is not possible to control every situation.
and i have tried hard with big.

keeping him close,
trying to always have him set up to succeed.

but no matter how careful a person is,
eventually there is a situation that spirals out of control.
there comes a day when the outcome is entirely in the hands
(or paws)
of the student.

it started out like any other day this "spring."
after a warm start, winter has been reluctant to leave.
march was colder than january.

as a result, we didn't have the explosion of spring this year.
instead buds have been swelling for weeks.
everything is ready, waiting for a little warm spell to explode.
today promised to start that long awaited change in the weather.

what today didn't warn us about
was that it was a test day for the big.

we barely came around the corner of the house
before big got his first chance to test his discipline.
there was a loud snort,
and a flash of white not 20 feet from us,
as we startled a white tail deer that had been browsing in the
yard.

we stopped and watched as he crashed off thru the woods.
big never even flinched.
"good job, mr big. but i bet you knew he was there all along."

a little later we came over a rise,
and spotted some black object in the road ahead.
as we got closer, the shape morphed into a big tom turkey

displaying.
he had found a fabulous stage in the road,
and he was strutting about proudly,
his tail fanned to its fullest,
and his beard stuck out like a flag.
three lady turkeys were standing beside the road,
watching and discussing him among themselves.

the group was so caught up in what they were doing,
that they didn't notice me and big
until we were close enough to see the hairs in his beard.
he stared at us for a moment,
then remembered who he was, dropped his tail,
and took off into the brush.
his lady friends started to follow, then hesitated
and took flight.

big held his discipline,
but he started pulling pretty hard....

we were close enough that he could have caught one before they
got off the ground,
and big still doesn't care for those sprinting ground buzzards.
i tapped his ear with my trainer,
to remind him that he was on the job.
"that's odd, big guy. we usually don't see only one male on
display."

a half mile later we saw a more normal setup.
three males were on stage in a hayfield,
surrounded by a bevy of beauties.

they stopped to watch us pass.
me and big stared back.
but this time he didn't pull.
big was on his best behavior today.
before we got home he was going to have to be.

we passed the misfit pack;
all five of them running in circles and barking from behind their
fence.
the big white dog sent a pee-mail and kicked up a rooster-tail.
big looked at them disdainfully and never broke stride.

the big year: winter and spring

(altho he did stop to answer the pee-mail after we got past their yard)
"good fella, mr big. you are one smart puppy."
big wagged his tail.
i think he was proud of himself.

big had passed his tests with flying colours.
but the truth was,
those had all been easy, multiple choice questions.
situations we have repeated a thousand times,
where big knew just what was expected of him.

i thought we were home free,
but the trick question was coming up.

crossing short creek,
we saw that the new family in the short creek house was out in the road.
they haven't been here long.
me and big know their schedules and routines,
but we don't know their names.

furthest from us was a little girl, about 7 or 8 years old.
she was playing catch with her dad,
who was about 20 feet closer to us.
obviously it was her first time ever to play catch,
and her throws rainbowed far off-line,
while her dad gave patient instructions.
another little girl, maybe 4 years old, was about 10 feet behind her dad...

and closest to me and big.

i was so immersed in watching the happy scene
of a family playing together outside,
that i wasn't really thinking of any potential issues.
big had dropped back beside me
(always shy around strangers)
and i just figured we'd walk past on the side of the road.
like everyone in the neighborhood,
the short creek family had seen me and big often enough.

the dad must have noticed the ballplayer looking at us,
because he turned to look.
then he started to walk towards the player,
while calling the younger girl to come with him.
i supposed they would huddle together while we passed....

me and big are used to that kind of thing.

but the younger child had her own ideas.
she took a few steps,
then turned, yelled "doggie!" and ran straight at me and big.

if there is one thing that scares big as much as bicycles,
it is someone running directly at him.
even what had to be the tiniest human he has ever seen.
the dad saw what was happening,
and turned to run after his young one, hollering at her to stop.
looking down,
i saw bigs eyes wide, and his tail tucked between his legs.
there were two people running directly at him now.
my mind raced thru my limited options;

i could let go of his leash and hope he ran away.
i remember how good he was at "catch me if you can."
the little girl would never touch him.
but dropping the leash is pretty much the least acceptable action
for a pit bull owner to take.

i could try to get between them,
or to cut the girl off.
but those would be unusual actions on my part.
and it all happened so fast, and she was so close.
there were only 3 or 4 seconds in which to respond.
what big did in those 3 or 4 seconds could determine if he would
live or die.

in my mind, altho i don't know what the experts would say,
the best course of action was to act like nothing was wrong.
if i showed disturbance,
that would only make it worse for the big.
"its cool, big fella."

the big year: winter and spring

the dad stopped running and calling.
he could see he would never catch her.
he just stared, with an odd blank expression on his face..
i imagine it was not the happiest moment in his life.

unaware of the crises unfolding all around her,
the little girl flung both arms around big's neck,
and laid her face against his.
big did not move a muscle.

we all stood that way for maybe 2 hours...

or maybe a few seconds.

it must have been a few seconds,
because i don't think anyone breathed.
then her dad called her again,
she let big go, and started towards her dad.

then she had a second thought.
the little girl turned and walked back to big
(who had still not moved a muscle)
grabbed a handful of the ample loose skin on either side of his face, leaned over him,
and planted a big kiss right in the middle of the top of his head.

this time the dad told her;
"that is enough petting *that* dog!"
and she went to join him.

big turned around facing the other way,
to let me know he'd rather go back the way we came.
"no, big guy, we don't have time to go back.
we're just gonna head to the house."

the man stood on the farthest edge of the road,
with his girls behind him,
as we passed.

i gave him a smile and;
"i guess that didn't turn out the way you expected?"
"no. not at all like i expected."

after we got around the corner, i told big;
"you done good mr big. you done real good."
he wagged his tail a little, but he didn't look up.
i think he was still a little shaken.
no telling what that tiny human could have done to him if i wasn't there.

laz

04-15-13
the big competition

so amy got even this morning.

me and big had kind of a late start walking,
and amy came driving up before we got a half mile down the road.
amy stopped beside us
and big stuck his head in the window for some petting,
then he went back to work.

that's how big is.
his work is important.

amy, however, did not go on her way.
she rode alongside me talking,
and as she did so,
she eased the bumper of her car in front of the big.

big did not look to either side,
he just increased his pace.
if that dog is anything, he is competitive.
i found myself being pulled down the road at an ever increasing speed.

"amy. you are making big crazy."
"i know."

"big. BIG! you can't race a car. well...
you can race a car. but you can't win."
big started to let up
(we go thru this every time a car stops to pet big,
and then pulls away)

instead of going on her way,
amy pulled out front of us,
slowed down and called out the window;
"big. i'm beating you, big... look who's in front!"
big set his eyes straight ahead,
and redoubled his pulling.

the big dog diaries

i could have put up a better fight,
except big looked so damn funny.
eyes fixed straight ahead,
pulling me down the road,
dead set on getting ahead of amy's car.

amy just laughed.

the girl has a mean streak.
she must have gotten that from her mother.
but on the whole
i think she was just trying to get even for yesterday.

yesterday
big and i were nearing the final mile when amy and sophie
caught up to us running.
i always hate it when amy and sophie pass us,
because big pulls until they are finally out of sight.
it kills his soul for another dog to pass him.
he is, after all, the number one dog.

on this particular morning,
amy was in a generous mood.
instead of passing and leaving me and big struggling in their
wake,
amy and sophe slowed down to walk it in with me and big.
the rest of the walk went well.
big likes having others along
(as long as he is in front)
but i hesitated when we reached the farm.
customarily big goes off leash the rest of the way to the house.
but customarily we don't have sophie along.
big likes to play with sophie....

a lot more than sophie likes big to play with her.

i decided to let him off and see how it went.
it went well.
big stayed in his usual position walking up the hill.
by the time we reached the house
i had forgotten all about my concerns.

the big year: winter and spring

big was trotting along a little ahead of us,
and when he reached the house...

he turned around and gave a kind of a hop.
i just had time to see a familiar gleam in his eye.
sophie must have seen it, too. she dropped to the ground.
big took off straight for sophie.
me and amy barely had time to respond at all.
but sophie did.
she knew what was coming,
big's great game called "leap over sophie"
just as big launched himself, sophie took off at right angles,
stretching her leash right in front of 100 pounds of hurtling,
airborne pit bull.

when big hit that leash,
amy and sophie both went airborne;
sophie unleashing a stream of pee,
amy unleashing a stream of profanity.
while i had to once again choke back laughter.

big made a couple more runs at the girls,
amy mixing in threats with the obscenities,
before he realized there was no fun to be had.

chastized, he retreated to the porch and went into his corner
behind the fireplace.

amy and sophie steamed past him,
still swearing and issuing threats.
after they went inside,
big came out of his corner and looked in the door,
wagging his tail sort of hopefully.

i was still waiting in the yard at the bottom of the steps.
"hey big."
he looked around.
"now that they're gone, do you want to play?"
big's face lit back up
he took one bound to the top of the steps and launched himself
right at me.

i gotta tell you;
seeing that hairy red cannonball airborne and coming right at
you is heartstopping;
even if he is grinning and laughing.
it was all i could do not to bolt like sophie did.
but i know the rules of bigsprints.
whatever you do, do not move!

his front feet hit about a foot in front of me,
and big shot off at a 45 degree angle.
nothing touched me except his backdraft.

while big was cutting a donut around my car,
i moved a few feet further from the porch.
that was really too close for my liking.

we played for a little while longer;
big making tight circles around the car, the dog pen, and in the
woods, punctuating each with a flying leap onto the porch, a 180,
and a flying leap back to the ground.

even with the extra room,
it was hard to hold position when big was flying straight at me.

before long big was huffing and puffing like a steam engine.
he is all athlete,
but a sprinter, not an endurance runner.
once he didn't have the steam to reach the porch in one bound,
the game was over....

i thought it was over.
at least it was over for that day.

half running down the road,
being towed by my big red tractor,
i could see amy laughing in her rearview mirror.

i thought to myself;
"NOW it is over."

these things are never really over until the woman gets the last
laugh.

laz

04-17-13
big birds

a flash of movement caught my eye.

me and big were resting after our morning's walk.
big was pooped out because the sumnmer heat came all at once,
and the leap from starting our mornings in the 20's and 30's
to having lows in the 60's and 70's
was pretty rough on my cold-loving friend.
i was pooped out because i have been stacking rock the last couple of weeks.
stacking rock is as close to real work as i ever care to get.
if big wasn't counting on me, i might have taken a couple of these days off.

so big and i were in full repose mode on the back porch,
big sprawled out on the cool stone,
me sunk into my chair.
and we weren't either one moving a muscle.

all i had to do to see the source of the movement was cut my eyes...

it was touch and go,
but i decided i had that much energy to spare.

a tiny wren was sitting about 3 feet away,
looking about nervously...
he turned his head this way and that,
to study me closely with his glittering little eyes.

he had a clump of dried grass in his beak.

obviously the little bird had selected a nesting site somewhere on the porch.

wrens get a bad rap around here.
they are more aggressive than the beloved bluebirds,
and tend to snatch the prime nesting sites in people's bluebird houses.

"just throw their nesting material out"
is the standard instruction for dealing with wrens.

well, me and big like wrens.
they are bright and alert, inquisitive and daring.
and they don't have a lot of friends.
nobody puts out food for them.
nobody builds them cute little houses...

"just throw their nesting material out."
me and big can identify.
he is too powerful, and too ugly.
i am too old.
society has cast the same vote against us.
i think there is room on the porch for one more reject.

i'm good at watching.
so that is what i did.
eventually the little bird decided it was safe,
and he flew down with his nesting material...

and took it inside my muddy boot, sitting beside the steps.

i guess i won't be wearing those boots for a while.
i wonder if they will be usable when the wrens are done?

me and big get a lot of pleasure out of the birds in big's territory.
and there are a lot of birds.
every morning at the first sign of predawn light the woods come to life.
countless songbirds celebrate surviving another night of predators,
and lay claim to their territories for another day.
woodpeckers hammer out a drumbeat to go with the music.

the chimney swifts chitter and thrum their wings as they get ready to head out for the day.
swifts are another reject sharing our porch,
their numbers in decline as the big old hollow trees have been gone for generations, and people put screen wire over the declining number of chimneys, to keep them out.

the big year: winter and spring

in the spring, when big starts looking up the chimney, i know the swifts are back,
and we will build no more fires.

soon the dog-food stealing nuthatch will be coming to check for food in big's bowl.
during the winter i pick up the crumbs big drops.
in the spring i leave them for his little friend to find.
and if he manages to pilfer a pellet now and then...

we can spare it.

turkeys gobble in the woods just out of sight,
sometimes we see the large flocks working their way across the yard, scratching and searching for food.

while we are walking, we come across the turkey theatres,
with the toms strutting, displaying and competing for the attention of an appreciative audience of hens.
soon the turkeys will seem to disappear,
as the hens hide out to brood their eggs.
when they next show up, they will be leading flocks of scrambling babies.

the short creek crows have been laying low lately,
but me and big are out every day,
walking and observing.
we are pretty sure there is a nest in the usual place down on ben's farm.

we haven't seen the local pair of redtail hawks in a while.
even tho it probably means they are also nesting,
and keeping a low profile,
we can't help but worry.
nature is beautiful, but it is life on the edge.
me and big will be watching.
if we are really lucky we will get to see another generation of arial acrobats
learning their craft over the pastures and fields of our little valley.

there are all kinds of birds around us.
finches, mockingbirds, bluebirds, and bluejays....

buzzards, sparrowhawks and even the rare squeaky gate bird.

there are more birds to see than we have time to see them,
each with their own habits and habitats.

this morning there was a new player in the bird game.
me and big saw a cooper hawk sitting in the big oak tree about
halfway down the drive.
life just got more exciting,
and the stakes even higher,
for all the birds on the big farm.
the oak tree may be his vantage point,
but the odds are we have cooper hawks nesting on the farm.

and the primary prey of cooper hawks are birds.

we have quite a summer ahead.

me and big feel sorry for people who live in the city.
how do they keep from getting bored,
when there is never anything exciting going on?

laz

04-19-13
big on duty

i have to remember to measure my words with big.
i can't just say anything that pops into my head,
because big takes my words to heart.

i'm sure we aren't the only people who have squirrel issues.
squirrels have their good points...

i think.

i suppose their mothers love them.

most people have a dichotomous attitude towards squirrels.
it is fun to watch them race thru the trees.
it is not fun to listen to them race thru the attic.
they are cute when they sit up and munch on hickory nuts and acorns.
they are not nearly as cute raiding gardens and bird feeders.

and they are not in any way welcome to share our vehicles.
sqirrels seem to have evolved for the express purpose of chewing wires and hoses.
if one of our cars sits unused for any time at all,
the squirrels turn it into a condominium.
they build nests in the nooks and crannies under the hood,
and hull nuts atop the air filter.
they stash food on top of the wheel wells,
and most of all they chew up the wires and hoses.

after a few painful repair bills, we have adapted.
sandra keeps a poisoned bait box next to her car,
one which the squirrels seem well aware is not safe for consumption...
as if killing the nearby squirrels would accomplish anything,
besides making space for immigrating squirrels.

we all chase them away from our cars when we see them,
altho that is mostly symbolic.
we do not scare the squirrels,

who merely scamper to a safe distance up a tree
and hang there, head down, scolding us.

and we keep track of when a car is parked.
even if we only drive to the mailbox and back,
every outside car has to be used regularly.
otherwise the squirrels will move in.

this is just the way things are living in the woods.

last week me and big were returning from our walk,
when big got distracted by my car.
at first i thought he was thinking i might want to go somewhere,
and he always thinks he should go with me.

then i noticed he was less interested in the passenger door
than he was in the hood.
as a matter of fact,
watching him,
he was sniffing at the grill,
sticking his head into the wheel wells,
and looking under the car.
it dawned on me that there was probably a squirrel in my car.
it had been parked a couple of days.

"is there a squirrel in my car, big guy?"
big wagged his tail and stayed focused on the car.

so i reached inside the car and popped the hood latch.
when i came around front to open the hood,
big was right with me.
he was on high alert,
watching intensely as i reached in for the release

as the hood raised,
a squirrel shot out the wheel well.
he only lived because of his head start...

big had to go around me, and the car,
but the big guy is unbelievably quick.
and i have to say, i have never seen a squirrel move so fast.
the squirrel went up the nearest tree,

the big year: winter and spring

big's jaws snapping shut with an audible "POP"
inches from his tail.

the narrow escape from death didn't go without notice.
the squirrel didn't even stop to scold us.
he kept going, leaping from tree to tree,
until he was far away.

"good boy, mr big. you can chase squirrels out of my car any time."
big came back wagging his tail and looking proud of himself.

in big's world there is no such thing as an offhand comment.
big now considers protecting our cars from squirrels as part of his job. when i am home he gets to stay on the porch.
now he divides his time between snoozing in his corner,
and patrolling our cars for any sign of squirrels.

the first thing he does when we get home from our walk is go from car to car,
checking all the wheel wells and sniffing at the grills.
squirrels might have snuck in while he was away.

the other day we came home and a squirrel was on the ground
between amy's car and the nearest tree.
big stomped both front feet on the ground,
and the squirrel took off.
big looked up at me proudly;
"good job, big fella."
big wagged his tail.

when you are a big,
there is a lot of responsibility.
he still knows not to chase squirrels in the woods.
but keeping them away from our cars has become a sacred trust.

we can rest a little easier now,
our issues with squirrels in our cars seem to be a thing of the past. we have a big on duty.

laz

04-25-13
a big's work is never done

we got out early today.
i knew that yet another cold wave was riding in on a line of rainstorms,
so after checking weather radar,
and seeing that we'd be cutting it close,
me and big were off into the darkness.

it was a nice morning, by my standards,
about 70, altho windy.
big would prefer freezing cold to go with the wind,
but heat does nothing to diminish his enthusiasm for our morning outings.
he greeted me with his wagging tail,
and a few of his amazing aerial maneuvers,
before sitting down so i could attach his leash.

with the seemingly endless string of cold fronts this year,
we were deprived of the dramatic spring opening that we enjoyed last year.
but nature won't wait forever,
and one by one the various trees and wildflowers gave up waiting on the warmth,
and everything has turned green.

me and big talked about this strange, cold spring as we walked along, the growing light unveiling the lush and picturesque hills of big territory under a threatening grey ceiling of scudding clouds.

as we approached home, we got hit by a few advance scouting parties of light rain,
but we hit the driveway dry, for all intents and purposes,
big getting to do the last stretch to the house with no leash.

about halfway up the hill, big started to pull ahead.
he finally got so far out front that i asked him;
"what's the rush, big guy?"

he stopped and turned around to wait for me, nervously shifting
his weight on his front feet.
there was trouble at the house and big knew it.
don't ask me how he knows these things,
but a big always knows.

as soon as i was close enough to see the house, big hurried on.
he went straight to my car and started circling it;
looking in the wheel wells,
and sniffing at the grill.
just as he suspected, a squirrel had taken advantage of his absence.

i finally got there.
"has a squirrel got in my car, mr big?"
big wagged his tail,
but never took his attention off the car.

i started to open the hood,
but the squirrel saw his chance when big was distracted,
and made a break for it.
as quick as big is (and big is unbelievably quick)
the squirrel reached the nearest tree with inches to spare.
big looked pretty smug as the squirrel made his desperate escape thru the treetops.
close encounters of the big kind put serious fear in any rodent.

big wanted to stay by the car,
but i convinced him to at least take a break to eat.
we had errands to run,
and i wanted to get as much done as possible before the rain arrived.

weather radar showed the leading edge of the storm almost on top of us, and the sky was growing darker by the second,
but we managed to make our stops at the dump and post office before the rain hit.

coming out of the post office,
i was met by loud peals of nearby thunder.
long thick columns of lightning stretched from the sky to the ground in the direction of the bank.
the edge of the storm was finally on us.

the big year: winter and spring

as i got in the car, large drops began to splatter on the windshield.

as we drove, the car was buffeted by the wind,
and sheets of rain turned the windshield opaque.
"we're probably going to have to do the drive-thru today, bigness."

big didn't show any sign he heard me.
he was in his usual riding position;
his elbow on the armrest and leaning against the door.
from there his powerful nose was directly in the breeze from the vent, and he could see out the windshield at the same time.

his focus did not waver, despite the poor visibility.
big knows our errand routines,
and we were heading toward the bank.
the bank is one of his favorite stops.

fate smiled on my big buddy.
just as we reached the bank, the rain dwindled to a sprinkle.
i looked at the big,
who was bouncing up and down with excitement...

"yeah, big fella. i think we can risk it."

the greetings met him at the door.
"look, it's big!"
"hello big!"
big led the way,
straight to the teller who hides dog biscuits in her drawer.
he put both front paws up on the counter,
then rested his chin on the counter between them,
his nose sticking thru her window.

she stroked his massive head and then gave him a dog biscuit.

the other teller borrowed a biscuit
and came out into the lobby to see the big.
he made himself available for some petting,
then she had him SIT
and held the biscuit in front of his nose.

the big dog diaries

his nose undressed the biscuit,
while he looked in her eyes and waited.

"OK"

the biscuit vanished.

before we left,
his lady friends gave big a ticket,
and i signed him up for a drawing.

knowing big, he'll probably win.
but if he does, we are splitting the money.
that's only fair...

i was the one who gave him a ride.

back on the road, we once again drove thru tornadic winds,
and sheets of rain.
at home, i made a mad dash for the porch,
telling big to come with me.
no need to make him wait in the rain.
i turned around to see him still at the car,
standing in the rain, checking the car for squirrels.

"big! come in out of the rain. no squirrels could get in the car
while we were driving."
big came up and went to lay in his corner.
he was due a nap,
we'd had a busy morning.

a little later, i looked out on the porch.
it was still pouring down rain,
but big's corner was empty.

i went out on the porch,
and there was my big dog...

soaking wet, standing in the cold rain;
guarding my car from squirrels....

a big's work is never done.

laz

04-26-13
the big furball

yesterday we started early to beat the rain.
today we started late to avoid the frosty cold.

i admit, it was me that wanted to avoid the cold.
arctic big loves it cold.

but the late start turned out good,
as we got to see some old friends that we had been wondering about. and opened up a whole new set of mysteries to ponder.

the bulk of our morning was spent on speculation.
nobody gambles more outside a casino than farmers.
around here there are several crops to choose between.
but the right choice can't be known until harvest time.

after last year's bumper wheat crop,
it seemed like most farmers had succumbed to the human belief that what happened before will happen again.
lots of wheat has been planted this year.
all the wheat, ben's included, has gotten off to a great start.
the cool spring hasn't bothered winter wheat one bit.

but other farmers have made different choices.
with so much wheat being planted, some speculated that prices won't be so good this year.
others are anticipating that what happened before won't happen again.
last year's corn was an unmitigated disaster.
this year it could as easily be the wheat.

this morning we walked past a couple of fields
one that had been wheat followed by soybeans last year,
and the other hay followed by soybeans.
neither had wheat this year,
and both were turning brown this week,
indicating that they have been herbicide sprayed preparatory to planting.
me and big think that means corn may be growing there this year.

we will know soon.
and if the weather is favorable this summer,
those cornfields will be things of beauty.

our morning miles passed by quickly,
talking about all the possibilities for the weeks ahead,
all the things we will get to see
once we start serious training for the meta mosquito 100km.
before we knew it, we were passing the lush green waves of ben's wheat,
and turning into the final mile home.

then we heard it;
"SKREEEE"

"hey big, the hawks are back!"
we hadn't seen or heard a hint of our local redtails in weeks.

"SKREEEE"
me and big walked along trying to home in on the source of the sound. i recognized the hoarser sound of the male.
i finally spotted his familiar shape sitting in a favored vantage point in a big hackberry tree.

but me and big were not the only ones homing in on his calls.
we didn't get to watch him but a few seconds before one of the short creek crows showed up.
this particular perch is only 500 or 600 yards from the crows' nesting site.
such proximity was not something the crows were going to tolerate.
after a couple of close flybys, the warrior hawk took wing.
he began effortlessly circling upward on an invisible column of air.

no wonder this was a favorite perch.
just as big and i have very different maps of the same territory;
me with my human roads and trails, big with the game trails and dog territories;
and the crows have maps of prime foraging sites and crow territorial boundaries;
the hawk no doubt has a map of thermals and hunting spots.

the big year: winter and spring

while me and big were pondering the multiple maps of our little valley,
each resident seeing the same land according to their own particular special lifestyle,
two more of the short creek crows showed up.

watching the crows diving onto the slow moving hawk,
i was reminded of fighter planes attacking a bigger, slower fighter-bomber.
the big hawk seemed only slightly perturbed as he continued to make effortless circles on his cushion of air.

in a couple of minutes i saw the princess female hawk gliding in from the east.
she joined her mate in the column of air,
and they both began spiraling slowly upward,
one making clockwise circles, the other counterclockwise,
greatly complicating the operations of the crows.
the last two short creek crows never put in an appearance.
me and big figured they were probably standing guard over the actual nest.
a suspicion somewhat confirmed later.
when we passed their nesting site on the border of the big farm and ben's place,
as we could hear them cawing to each other in the woods.

in the meantime we got a surprise.
a pair of big buzzards came gliding in to join the fray.
"we got us a regular furball, big guy."
the thermal was now clearly visible, delineated by the circling birds.
it was easy to imagine the circling birds as engaging in a dogfight;
the huge buzzards like big bombers, the mid-sized hawks as fighter-bombers, and the little crows as fighters.

watching all the birds circling, maneuvering, and diving in such a confined space,
the term "furball" for a mass of dogfighting planes made perfect sense.
it was remarkable to see so many birds in such a small space, and no collisions.

the tangle of birds didn't last long.
the addition of the buzzards made it too tight for the crows,
and the trio soon broke off the engagement
(interestingly enough, they left in the opposite direction from their nest)
after the crows left, the two hawks changed their tactics.
instead of circling in opposite directions they fell into tandem,
rode the air current up high,
and then glided off to the north together.
only the pair of buzzrds remained,
and they quietly floated up the air elevator,
before heading back the way they had come.

me and big had come to a stop while we watched the whole exchange taking place.
but observation can leave you with more questions than answers.
"so, big, do you think the hawks and buzzards are allies against the crows?"
one thing was certain.
nothing we had watched was just random chance.
the crows worked together to drive off the hawks.
the hawks worked together to make it difficult for the crows to attack.
and the buzzards....

the buzzards changed the whole dynamic.
but why?

"you know what, mr big? birds are complicated."

big just turned up the road so we could get started again.
i'm not sure what it all means (yet) but that was quite a show.
lucky for me and big we decided to start late this morning.

laz

05-08-13
the big vet visit

yesterday was a big day for the big dog.
it was time for his annual checkup at the vet.

big loves to go to the vet....
maybe even more than he loves to go to the bank.
so it was no surprise when he began wagging his tail as soon as we turned towards the vet's office.
unfortunately, big gets to see the vet more than once a year;
a byproduct of his big lifestyle.

i made him WAIT at the door while i stuck my head in,
so i would know what the situation was inside before we went in.
we were good.
there was only one person in the waiting room,
a man with a small crate,
and he was not right next to the door.

as soon as big came in, he set his eyes on the crate,
the intensity of his look plainly indicated there was a cat inside.
but he had to make time to go and greet the lady at the desk.
he has his public to think of.
his favorite, kaycee, was not in her usual place.
big wanted to go looking for her,
and he wasn't happy when i told him we had to sit and wait.
he alternated between staring at the cat,
and whining at the door to the back.

when i asked about kaycee, the news was not good.
she was a student at mtsu,
and had to quit at the vet's office to do an internship.
last time kaycee was not there, we had to go back the next day,
so he could see her.
that wouldn't be an option this time.
big will be looking for her for a long while.
in big's world people sometimes leave and never come back.

he never gets used to that.

the first order of business was getting big's weight.
usually he treats this as a fun game,
called "never stop on the scales."
the trick is to happily obey every command,
"HOP UP", "SIT"
but never end up sitting on the scales.
"no, don't get back on the floor, you silly goober. SIT on the scales"
big grinning like an idiot, his eyes twinkling with mischief.
this time he just hopped on when i told him to,
and SAT as requested.

when his weight was down to only 90 pounds,
i felt good about it.
must be a runner thing.
i attributed it to us ramping up our training pace to get ready for the met-a-mosquito 100k.
i should have known better.
big never loses weight by training.
he just packs on more muscle.

when our turn came to go to the examining room,
big had to be convinced that our mission was not to look for kaycee.
but once we were there,
he settled in and watched the crack at the bottom of the door.
the vet would be coming to see him next.
big is a happy dog when he knows the drill.

i hope the other dogs never tell big that drawing blood and giving him two shots is not petting.
because he, as usual, greeted the vet with a wagging tail,
and assumed the position for his eagerly awaited affection.
afterwards, the big beamed as the vet patted his head, and told him;
"you *are* a good dog."

on the way back out to the waiting room,
big had to be convinced again,
that we were not there to locate kaycee.
if we were smart,

we'd have just gone on out the door and went home.
but we had to wait on the results of big's blood test.

the waiting room turned into grand central station,
as a stream of people and pets came in...

i think they had scheduled every person in the county that fears pit bulls.

a lady came in with a small dog.
i had big's leash rolled around my hand so he couldn't go anywhere, but he stood up, faced the door, and wagged his tail at her as she came in.
big feels like he is the official greeter when he is at the vet's office.

the woman gasped, and went right back out.
after a few moments, she came back in
staying as far from big as possible she came in and sat down.

after a few minutes she finally looked at big.
he wagged his tail.
she said;
"that is a big dog."
we talked for a little before she asked;
"is he safe to pet?"
"yes, he thinks that is what we are here for."
she stroked the top of big's head;
big closed his eyes and wagged his tail.

the lady and her dog went into the back,
and it wasn't 30 seconds before a man came in with a huge tom cat wearing a cone.
the man apologized to the lady at the desk for not having a crate;
"he is too big for my crate."
they brought him a dog crate and he put the cat inside.

when he sat the crate on the floor,
the cat came over and sat looking out at big.
big had not taken his eyes off the cat since it came in the door.

the man asked if big was a pit bull.
i always hate that question.

it doesn't seem like the breed of the dog is really what it is about.
it is about what kind of dog, and dog owner, we are.
i gave the usual answer;
"yeah... but he is a good natured dog."

so the man told me about his cat.
it had been attacked by a dog...
or maybe a coyote.

i looked at his cat, staring out at big (who was staring back)
the cat's face looked like it had been thru a shredder.
one ear was completely gone.
to be perfectly honest, that did not resemble dog damage at all.
(unless the dog used a switchblade)

while i was contemplating that, they called the man back.
he got up, and before he picked up the crate he hesitated
and asked;
"is he safe to pet?"
"he thinks that is why we are here. he loves to be petted."
the man stroked big's head cautiously.
big closed his eyes and wagged his tail.

the next visitor was a huge man,
probably 6-5 and at least 300 pounds.
he only hesitated for a moment when he saw big.
then he headed for the same seat as everyone else...
the furthest seat from big.

he was there to pick up his dog that had been spayed.
while he waited he told me his brother had a dog like big.
it was as gentle and affectionate as could be...

until it was told to attack.
then it would destroy whatever it was set on.
it had made his brother a lot of money fighting.
"after the other dog is dead, you have to pry his jaws open to get
him loose."

just then they brought his dog in.
it was some sort of long-haired toy dog, must have weighed 4
pounds. he left without asking to pet big.

the big year: winter and spring

i think big was as glad of that as i was.
he was the first person to come in that did not get a big tail wag.

bigs know.

then a woman came in with an ancient chihuahua.
she eased around out of reach,
then took the next seat down from us.
she looked at big and smiled. big wagged his tail.
big and the lady flirted for a few more minutes,
then she asked;
"is he safe?"
"he's a good natured dog. he loves people."
she petted that broad head,
and big sat down, wagging his tail.

no sooner had the chihuahua lady started for the back
than the door opened and a heavyset woman stepped in.
she took one look at big and all the color drained from her face.
she backed out and shut the door behind her.

me and big waited.
finally the door opened very slowly.
the heavyset woman, and an equally heavyset man eased their way inside.
each was holding a tiny puppy, and had their eyes fixed on big.
i think if he had farted,
they'd have torn down the door getting out.

they sidled along the wall to the furthest possible seat,
and sat without ever taklng their eyes off big.
big just sat at my feet, doing nothing.
i don't even think little would expect any petting from those two.

apparently they were new patients, and had to fill out the new patient forms.
the woman was so fixated on big that she was struggling.
the lady at the desk came over to us,
she leaned over and said;
"you're a good dog, big."
then she petted him and scratched behind his ears.
big wagged his tail.

she didn't say so,
but i think she was trying to ease the petrified people's fear.

then it got comical.
one by one, the previous patients started coming out.
each one said;
"goodbye, big."
all of them but the cat guy gave big a pat on the head.
(and he had an armload of one-eared cat-that had been in a knife fight with a dog)

the petrified people must have been wondering if they were on candid camera;
all these crazy people petting a deranged killer dog.

then the vet came out and came over to me and big.
he scratched big behind the ears while he talked to me.
"big came up clean on heartworm...

but he tested positive for a tick-borne disease, ehrlichiosis."

big was wagging his tail. the petrified people were watching.
"has he been sluggish lately? or sleeping a lot?"
i racked my brain.
he had been sleeping a lot, and he had been dragging a little at the end of a couple of our walks.
but i had attributed it to the warmer weather.
he hadn't played big sprints since the day he sent amy and sophie airborne.
and he did get on the scales today without playing his goofy game.
"they lose weight"
dam. an hour ago i was proud of his weight loss.
"it causes inflammation in the joints. sometimes dogs get down in their legs."
i had seen big stumble and limp some.
but i thought it was from where he got shot.
i felt like a failure as a master.
my big guy trusts me.
and i had let him down.

i was feeling sorry for my boy while the vet told me i needed to come pick up medicine for the big on thursday.

"he'll have to take it for 4 weeks. it is important that he takes the whole course."
"is it flavored where dogs will like it?"
"i don't know for sure. maybe you'll have to disguise it."
"that's not so easy. big is very clever."
"you can put it in something good."
"i've been thru this with his last medicine. i have to come up with a new trick every two or three doses. big is very clever."

i sat there contemplating all this while they packaged up the three months of heartworm stuff for big.
it depleted his entire fund.....

his entire fund. oh crap.
"how much is this medicine going to cost?"
the lady at the desk looked it up for me...

it was 6 weeks of grocery money.
the shock must have shown on my face because she quickly told me;
"we can break it down to weekly, and make the payments less."
"no. that's ok. i'll figure it out."

as i was going out the door, the petrified man finally spoke;
"you can never trust a pit bull" he told me.

me and amy talked about it this morning.
"poor big" she said.
it is hard to think about our happy dog feeling bad.
he makes us all laugh and feel good.

just before amy left for work she gave me a piece of paper.
"will this help?"
it was a check, and very nearly covered big's medicine.

sometimes our children really make us proud.

laz

05-10-13
the big laugh

i have to start by saying that i understand dogs do not have a
sense of humor.
at least not a sense of humor like we humans display
(ok. most of we humans)

they have a sense of play.
they can even laugh;
a breathy "ha-ha-ha" that they make when they play.
if there was any doubt that is a dog version of laughter,
all you have to do is make that sound...

and see if your dog doesn't respond by wanting to play.

dogs don't have a sense of humor,
and that is how we know it was in all innocence
when big came quietly up behind amy in the dark
and bumped his nose into her leg...

eliciting her own version of the spontaneous leap,
accompanied by a scream.

dogs just don't have the brainpower to drive a real sense of
humor. that's how i know this morning was also pure innocence.

weather radar revealed
that rain was only minutes away,
so we postponed our walk for later.
i needed to make a quick run to the christiana market anyway,
so i figured i would do it now and take big with me as
compensation.
not that big would willingly let me go without him.
he feels like it is his job to wait on the porch,
and accompany me any time i leave the house.

i went out on the porch and broke the news to big.
" no walk this morning, big guy; it's about to start raining.
do you want to go to the store instead?"

the big year: winter and spring

big ran down the steps and went out to wait by the passenger door of my car.
i have about quit trying to figure out how he knows these things.
i know dogs can't speak english.

now, we have a routine for getting in the car.
i let big in the passenger door,
and he sits in the passenger seat and waits while i go around and get in the driver's side.
that is our normal routine.
but big was feeling his wheaties this morning.
i opened the door.
"ok, mr big. hop in."
he hopped across, sat in the drivers seat, and looked at me with a twinkle in his eye.
i know that twinkle well.
it is the sense of humor that dogs don't have.
what better joke could a dog play
(if a dog had a sense of humor)
than to obey every command, without doing what you want?

"get back over here, big. that's my seat."
big hopped back to the passenger side and stood there looking at me.
"you have to sit down, or i can't close the door."
big hopped back over to the driver's seat, and sat down.
"no, big fella. you were supposed to sit over here."
big gave me that innocent look.
"i'm just a dumb old dog. i don't know what you want."
"you silly goober. come over here and sit."
big hopped into the passenger side of the back seat and sat down.
his face was lit up with merriment. if he could produce tears,
they would have been rolling down his cheeks.
"all right, you goofy dog. get back up here and sit in the front."
big hopped back in the driver's seat, and sat down...

big can't laugh out loud.
but i can.

laz

05-12-13
really?

ok. i was wrong again.
big sure could have chosen a better master.

after two days of doxy,
the big guy is like a new dog.
i thought after four or four and a half years
he was finally slowing down a little bit....

nope.
the old big is back.
this morning he was standing at my feet,
wagging his tail in anticipation.
i picked up his leash and he launched himself in a patented big spontaneous leap.
his spontaneous leaps had been only about shoulder high.
this one got him high enough to look me square in the eye.

it is wonderful to have the old big back.
we had a great workout/walk this morning.

but after we got back,
i faced the same old problem.
every dose of medicine is a fresh challenge.

the pills were advertised as "chicken flavored."
someone forgot to tell the big.

when i came out with his first round,
he readily bought into the "treat" approach.
he SAT at my feet eagerly,
licking his lips in anticipation.

i held out the two pills in my palm
and gave him the OK.
the pills vanished.

two seconds later they dropped on the porch;
with a wet "plop-plop"

the big dog diaries

big looked at my hand to be sure there had not been a mistake,
then he started to walk away with a look of betrayal.

while his back was turned, i slipped them into his food bowl,
and called him back.
that first round went down as if he didn't even notice the pills.
i could only hope it would continue to be that easy.

it did not.

each successive round, i have had to get more clever.
the next time he was sure i had something hidden there,
and he ate around the pills.

as soon as they were exposed, and pushed aside,
i reached in his food bowl
and pushed the now slobbery pills back under a pile of food.
the second time the soggy pills stuck to the food,
and down they went again.

after that it became an arms race;
big getting ever more deft at segregating the pills...

me getting ever more devious in re-hiding them.

this morning big decided to try a new approach.
he SAT and i placed his bowl on the ground.

i gave the OK and he came over for his usual pre-meal petting;
placing the broad top of his head against my leg,
giving me ready access to his ears and neck.

but, instead of going to his food bowl after the petting,
he went over and lay down on his bed...

and looked at me.

"i think i'll just wait till you go inside to eat.
otherwise you are going to make me eat those pills."

i was in something of a quandary.
big is not sophie (whose food would have been gone before you could think about petting her)

the big year: winter and spring

big is not little (who would eat her food if it had turpentine in it)
big can be darn patient when he has a goal.

and i didn't have all day.
we were supposed to take my mother to buffet for mothers day.
when it came time to go,
i wasn't about to tell sandra i was engaged in a battle of wits and will with the big.
she would tell me to give up...

i didn't stand a chance.

but i am not near as dumb as sandra thinks i am.
(heck, i think i am smarter than the average dog)
i still had a trick or two up my sleeve.

i remembered in the past,
when big decided to save his meal for later,
if he saw little or sophie so much as look at his bowl,
he was on it, and eating, in two shakes of a lamb's tail.

so i opened the back door and called;
"LITTLE!"

i didn't have to call twice.
little is always ready to go outside with me
and do anything i want to do.

little came at a dead run,
and screeched to a halt in the doorway,
with her head sticking out.

she looked at big's bowl of food.

she looked at big;
who was now sitting at alert,
watching her with an intently fixed stare.

then she looked at me with her saddest eyes,
her ears folded down against her head.
"uh. no thanks. i'll just wait in here until later...

like after big eats later."

"it's ok little. you don't have to go near his food.
just come out on the porch, and then you can go back inside."

i swear, little looked at me incredulously.

"really? REALLY? you want to use me as a bait dog?"

little backed back into the house,
then turned and walked away
(watching me over her shoulder)
i suppose she didn't want to risk being dragged out there.

fortunately, that was enough to do the trick.
(this time)
big came over and scarfed his food down,
he was in such a hurry
that i only had to relocate his pills once.

and i am sure little will forgive me.
dogs don't bear grudges.
so all is well that ends well...

except i only have two days down.
four doses.

28 days remain.
56 doses.
112 pills.

i can do this.
i know i can.
i am, after all, smarter than the average dog.

of course my opponent is the big,
not the average dog.
the shelf life of each trick is approximately one dose.

i have a feeling this is going to require the determination of a
barkley finisher.

laz

05-14-13
hey-hey, boo-boo

i don't want you to think big is engaged in a battle of wits with an unarmed man.

i tried a whole new tactic tonight.
i painted his pills lightly with peanut butter,
then hid them at the very bottom of his food.

big stood there sniffing a moment,
nothing gets past that nose of his.
then he dug them out and gobbled them down.
i swear he almost looked smug.

"there's no fooling you, big guy."

with that first victory in hand,
big lay down to polish off the rest of his meal.

as yogi would say;
"i'm smarter than the average dog."
and once in a while i get one over on the big, too.

laz

05-15-13
the big shape-shifter (part 1)

every morning when my eyes pop open,
i am ready to go.
there is a treat waiting for me.

now that he has moved to the porch,
big no longer greets my opening eyes with frantic barking
(i think amy is glad he has moved)
but that doesn't mean he isn't ready.
there is no need to bark.
if i go out a door,
big will be there.

it takes a little longer to loosen up my old bones,
but my mind is ready.

the first thing i do is peek out the window at big's nest.
sometimes he is only a shape in the dark,
but i know what i would see if it was light.

big is lying there with his head on his front paws...

looking back at me.

we don't have to see each other to know.

the next thing i do is go out for the morning greeting.
i don't want to make him wait.
big greets me each morning,
as if he had heard that i died in my sleep.

he hurries over and leans that great head against my leg,
tail wagging,
his eyes alight with joy;
"oh, thank god, you're alive!"
"sweet heaven, it's a miracle, YOU ARE ALIVE!!"

once we get past that initial thrill,
i go back inside to get ready for the day.
big follows my progress thru the windows.

the big dog diaries

when i put on my shoes,
big is practically hopping up and down;
"ohmygod, ohmygod, he's coming back out. any minute now he's coming back out!!!"

when he see's me carrying his food bowl,
the impossible happens....

he gets even more amped up;
"FOOD? there is going to be food, too? how can life be so good."

once i reach the porch,
he is much more restrained.
the stakes are high.
he has to do everything just right.
as i set his bowl on the table, i can see that big nose going,
checking to see if there is a special treat today;
"sweeeet... peanut butter."

(i am so glad i taught master to bring me peanut butter when he wants me to take a pill)

but it isn't the food that has his focused attention.
there is something way more important than food at stake.

i pick up his leash,
and 100 pounds of muscle and sinew launches into the air.
the competing forces of velocity and gravity reach equilibrium just at head height,
and for that split second, our eyes meet.
then the big rocket returns to earth with a thud.

this is no easy maneuver,
for he has to adhere to strict rules.
bigs are not allowed to jump actually on people.

one day last week, his front paw hit my thigh on the way down.
big was mortified.
he SAT so fast it almost seemed like he landed on his butt.
(usually he has to be reminded to SIT while i hook up his leash)
"what was that about, big fella?"
"ididntmeanto, ididntmeanto"
(sometimes it is really hard to enforce the rules...

like when you are looking into that sincerely horrified face)
"you know the rules"
i set down his leash and started back for the house.
the rule is; if a big jumps on someone, they walk away.
can any punishment top that?

i turned to walk away
and big scooted around me on his butt at top speed,
looking for all the world like an old-timey movie in fast motion.
he cut me off before i reached the door,
looking up pleadingly.
he scooted backwards in front of me all the way to the door,
somehow even sliding his butt up onto the step,
without raising up.
then he scooted over to give me room to go inside.

i went in, shut the door,
then i opened it up and came back out.
big is a dog, and dogs only have one time;
"now."
there is no need to punish them forever.
i punished him "now"
and once i closed the door,
it was a different "now."

if i did not come back out, it wouldn't be punishment.
it would mean i hated him.
and no one wants a depressed big on their porch.

but today i wasn't worried about a depressed big.
i was concerned about a different big altogether.

the past few days there had been a new resident at the pug
house. from who-knows-where they had added a large white
male pyrhenies to their menagerie.
i was already concerned this would cause problems with the big
(this is what happens when you have neighbors only a quarter
mile away)
but yesterday when i came home from stacking rocks,
the pyrhenies was in our driveway at the bottom of the hill.

i knew big was not going to like that.
not liking it turned out to be an understatement.

the big dog diaries

we reached the place where i had seen the other dog,
and big stiffened.
then he drew himself up to his full 23 inches,
and got as big as he could get.

big is really pretty amazing in his varied configurations.
when he is out on his cable,
jumping around and begging me to let him off
(an odd thing, since he can take off his cable at will)
he seems to compress into what case refers to as;
"half dog, half beer keg."
his bulging eyes (probably from pulling his collar so tight)
and maudlin, panting grin,
give him a pig-clown appearance.

when we walk, he often has his head low and out front,
swinging it from side to side,
sampling the air.
between his rolling walk,
thick body,
round face, and short muzzle,
i feel like i am walking a small, red bear.

and sometimes, he just looks like a dog
(until you get an angle that reveals just how thick he is)

but his number-one-dog posture is my favorite.
he is like a middle aged man at the beach,
sucking in their gut and puffing out their chest;
except big actually achieves the effect he is shooting for.
stretching for every inch of his limited height,
head held proudly high,
he is magnificent.
wide hips and powerfully muscled thighs;
compact (if not actually thin) waist;
then expanding sharply in a classic "V"
to shoulders that seem to be composed of mountain ranges of muscle.
with his head erect,
that huge hump of muscle at the base of his neck spreads across
his shoulders, adding layers of muscle on top of layers of muscle.
then his thick, tebow neck blends into this outsized head.

a deep seam runs down the center of the wide, flat top of his head.
at the bottom of that seam is actually a high ridge of bone on the top of his skull.
it is simply buried in thick sheets of muscle.
and that funny looking round face,
is nothing but more muscle,
all attached to one of the widest mouths in the dog world.
the big, when he wants to, looks like just what he is;
a perfectly designed biting machine.

add those cold yellow eyes...

someone called them "wolf eyes" the other day,

and you have one very impressive
(some might say downright scary looking)
dog.

once you get used to them, his eyes do show expression.
they show affection, joy, humor...

this morning the expression was that of a linebacker on steroids, preparing to blitz the quarterback who stole his girlfriend.

05-15-13
vegas knows their stuff

i think the over under was 4 feedings?

this morning was the 4th feeding.
i was starting to feel smug.
big did his scavenger hunts like it was a party game.

yesterday gave me a little scare.
when big ate the second pill he hesitated.
then he worked his mouth around...

and dropped out two of the food pellets that had been glued to the pill with peanut butter.

this morning he quickly located the first "prize"
but part way thru eating it he looked unhappy.
he messed around for a moment,
but it was apparently already too chewed up to reject.

the second pill he took in his mouth,
and after a little working around,
dropped a perfectly clean pill back in his bowl.

there was no persuading him to eat it.

i got a thick piece of baloney (about a half inch square),
slit it and put the pill inside.

he eagerly took the baloney.

and after a few seconds dropped a clean pill in his bowl.

i went and got a little cheese.

big was waiting when i came back out.
this new game was fun!

but i was not beaten yet.

the big dog diaries

when i held out the cheese treat,
i held it up high.
big had to stretch his neck to reach it.

at the same time i gave him the OK to make it vanish,
i reached over with my other hand and blocked him from putting his chin back down.

i could see him strip the treat from the pill
(or at least i could see the tell-tale motions of his mouth)
then he tried to lower his head to drop out the pill....

HA!
no matter how smart you might be,
it takes real lips to spit!

he had no choice but to swallow.
he had a mouthful of cheese.
if he didn't swallow soon,
he would drown in saliva.

so i don't know who wins.
the over/under was 4.

big defeated the hidden peanut butter trick at the midpoint of the 4th dose.

laz

05-17-13
The big shape-shifter (part 2)

while we finished the last part of the driveway
i considered changing our route for the day.
big was sniffing at various "message posts" along the way
and growing ever more incensed.
the ridge of hair down his back bristled
and his eyes were fairly crackling.

obviously he did not like the pee-mails he was receiving.

we were planning to do fosterville road.
but that would take us past the pug house...

twice

on the other hand,
this was not a confrontation that could be avoided forever.
there are only two directions to choose at the end of the driveway.
between loop courses and out-backs,
some 75% of out routes go past the pug house.
i was not throwing away 75% of our choices.
we might as well deal with the dog sooner,
rather than later.

it was just as well that i planned to go that way.
usually big kind of watches at the end of the drive,
to see which way we are going.
this morning he took the right turn without asking.

i was looking at big,
while we closed the distance to the pug house.
he was still in his hercules configuration,
walking with very deliberate strides.
his appearance, his posture, his whole attitude
all fairly screamed that he was a large, powerful, and dangerous dog.

when we reached the pug house,
i did not see the pyrhenies at first.

then it walked out from behind a car
and stood looking at us.
big turned and made a beeline for it.
he did not growl or bark.
he did not charge.
he just headed straight for this usurper.
big is the number one dog, and he had a bone to pick with this newcomer.

no one is coming to big's yard
and declaring themself the number one dog.
that job is taken.

it took some doing to finally drag big past the pug house.
and then we had to stop about five times in the next hundred yards for big to send angry pee-mails
and kick up great clots of dirt and grass.
the white dog merely watched us.

i was left to brood as we headed into the hills towards fosterville.
this was not a good situation.
trouble was bound to happen with big and the new pyrhenies;
big is difficult (perhaps impossible) to contain.
and the pug house people were certainly not going to make any effort to contain their dog.
the only dog they have ever restrained is the insane pit bull.
and that was only because it was killing all their cats.
getting killed in the road,
biting people,
or otherwise presenting a nuisance,
are dog behaviors to which the pug family is indifferent.
it has been no problem keeping big from going to the pug house.
but the pyrhenies was already coming to our house.
trouble was brewing.
altho the white dog was considerably larger than big,
big is designed to be an agent of destruction.
for their dog's part, pyrhenies are also designed for trouble.
they guard flocks from canine predators.
an encounter between the two contending number one dogs
would likely not be good for either one.

the big year: winter and spring

as we approached the home of the misfit pack,
i saw the owner out loading stuff into the back of his pickup.
i could see the aussie dog, and the two tribbles.
but their big white pyrhenies was no where to be seen.
he had taken to not being in the yard,
preferring to be out with their cattle.
but we usually saw him.
big and i had found it amusing
watching the piles of rock spring up around their yard fence
as they tried to plug the places the white dog dug his way out.

lucky for them, they did not own a big.
big would not find a need to dig out,
as he could hop over that 4-foot fence at will.

then a thought came to my mind, unbidden.
"hey, big. have we seen their white dog recently?"
big didn't say anything,
but he already knew the answer.

i stopped at the driveway and hollered to the man loading his truck; "HAS YOUR BIG WHITE DOG GONE MISSING?"
he stopped and looked at me and big.
"YES! HE'S BEEN GONE FOR 3 DAYS."
"WELL, I THINK I KNOW WHERE HE IS."

the man came over,
and i told him about the new dog at the pug house.
and he told us the white dog's story:
"he wasn't actually our dog, he belonged to a friend,
who used him to guard his goats. then he got sick.
he got so bad he wasn't able to watch the goats.
so we took him in."
(this explains why the first time we saw him, he didn't even stand up)
"after he got better
we couldn't even keep him in the yard."
i laughed; "me and big have been watching the piles of rock grow around your fence."
"yeah, as fast as we plug one hole, he dig's another.
all he wants to do is stay with the cows."
(if men had the work ethic of dogs,

no job would ever be half done)
"anyway, last week one of the cows got down.
he stayed with it for a couple of days.
we did what we could, but finally we had to shoot it...

the dog was heartbroken.
he stayed with the cow's body for two days.
he refused to even eat, then he disappeared."

"he must have felt betrayed!"

john, as the man had introduced himself,
asked for directions to millersburg road.
he had some work to do on his farm,
but first he was going to see if that was his dog
that had moved into the pug house.
i sure hoped it was.

big and i continued our patrol
up into the fosterville hills.
an hour later we came back by...

there in the front yard with the rest of the misfit pack
(at least for the time being)
was a big white pyrhenies.
"you knew it was him all along, didn't you big?"
big didn't answer.
he was busy ignoring the big white dog,
while it raged and barked,
sent pee-mails, and kicked up rooster tails...
from behind its own fence.

once we were past and down the road,
big stopped to issue his own pee-mail response.
then he kicked a fantail of dirt into the road.
big looked over his shoulder to make sure the pyrhenies had seen him.
then he looked up at me.

i am pretty sure that big was grinning.
all was right in big territory.

laz

05-26-13
big the baloney hound

the big has always looked at medicine as some cool game i thought up.
my objective is to get the medicine in.
big's objective is to keep it out.

i'm a clever guy.
(smarter than the average dog)
as fast as big mastered one method,
i'd come up with another.
but big is not your average dog.
big learned that i would coat pills with peanut butter,
or melt them in cheese.
i learned that a dog can remove pills cleanly from peanut butter and melted cheese.
i figured out that dogs can't spit.
big mastered moving pills to the tip of his tongue,
and flipping them backwards over his head.

i finally had to go to the last resort.
i pried that alligator mouth open,
shoved the pills to the back,
and then held it shut until he swallowed.

me and big have been thru too much.
i knew he wouldn't bite off my hand.

what i hadn't considered was saliva.
with a mouth big enough to fit my entire head,
and a tongue the size of a handtowel,
inserting a pill got me wet halfway to my elbow.
and it was not a pleasant wet.
there is nothing quite so slimy as dog slobber.

i went back to hiding the pills in various foods.
then, quite by accident,
i found big's weakness....

that dog loves baloney.

he *really* loves baloney.

he does not like having me stick my arm down his throat.

so me and the big have reached a compromise.
i feed him his pills in a slab of baloney.
and he eats them.
he knows they are in there,
but if he gets his baloney, he eats them.
now, this is not a simple deal.
he expects a certain amount of baloney in exchange for eating the pills.

if his slab of baloney is inadequate....

he removes the pills and drops them back in his bowl.
then he gives me that look.
"i don't want your arm down my throat any more than you do...
but it was you that cut that puny piece of baloney."

i didn't have to wash my arm but so many times.
before i figured out what size slab of baloney the big expects.

laz

05-26-13
big rehab

there are certain concepts that dogs just don't get.
nasty comes to mind.
dogs may have a thousand words for "crinkle"
but they have no word for "nasty."
the result is a certain lack of discrimination
when it comes to eating and drinking.

another concept almost wholly lacking in dogs is "careful."
big does show some caution when meeting strange people.
that is the extent of his safety program.
beyond that the big enters every situation headfirst...

and full bore.

the result of this
is being on a first-name basis with everyone at the vet's office.

big being on a first name basis.
i am just his transportation.

and so i made a call to the vet's office last week.
"this is 'laz'"
silence
"big is my dog."
"oh, and what is up with the big today?"
"he seems to have sliced one of his toe pads in half,
and nearly cut off his dewclaw.
i wasn't sure if i should bring him in, or if it will heal on its own."
"is it bleeding?"
"it must have bled, because there is blood all over the back porch.
but it isn't bleeding now."
"well, then just bandage it up and keep him off of it a few days.
it will probably heal on its own."
"ummm. this is the big. he doesn't wear bandages...
and he has some miles scheduled right now.
big does not believe in taking days off."
"if he limps too bad, or it starts bleeding again,
he might have to take some days off."
"i'll watch him close."

the big dog diaries

big has only one approach to rehab.
whatever the injury, you work thru it.
he limped pretty bad on the large gravels in the driveway.
but he had no interest in turning back.
by the time we reached the smooth road surface,
he was walking as if nothing was wrong.
i was watching his tracks for blood.

when it came time for him to send a pee-mail, we stopped.
"i guess you won't be kicking up any rooster tails this morning,
huh big guy?"
good thing i didn't bet.
as soon as his pee-mail was complete,
big dug in with all four feet,
and kicked a spray of dirt out behind him.
i could see him stagger,
as he pulled and thrust out a great clod of dirt and grass with his injured foot.
it made me wince, to think of that bisected pad digging in thru the dirt,
and tearing that fresh wound open again.
i quickly pulled him back on the road with his leash,
because he was undeterred, getting ready for his second kick..

by the time he had sent a few pee-mails, i was ready every time.
big seemed incapable of learning that it would hurt like heck
to kick up a rooster tail...

or else he simply did not care.

i remembered back when he first showed up, shot.
the vet said she hoped it could heal without surgery...

"this kind of dog makes poor surgical patients.
they do not slow down for rehab."

she called that one right.
so each morning, me and big have done his "rehab."
he gets up and hobbles over to get his leash on,
and his limp gradually decreases as we walk.
not one workout has been cut short.
the only thing is, i won't let him kick up rooster tails.
and the big method of rehab seems to work.

the big year: winter and spring

this morning he scarcely limped at all.
the two halves of the pad have been healing from the bottom and the edges. hardly any red meat is still showing in the cut.

little has her own approach to rehabbing an injury.
i have to go do chores right now,
but later on i will share the tale of;
"little and the cone of shame..."

laz

06-07-13
big beta site

yesterday morning, when me and big started our walk,
it was the darkest of darks.
i was expecting it to be dark,
as we knew from the previous mornings that the moon was either new,
or within a day of the new moon.
we have been watching it shrink to a sliver.
but yesterday morning was inky black.
not even the light of a single star gave form to the shadows.

fortunately, me and big have our routine down until we don't need light.
he came over and nuzzled my leg,
so i could stroke that broad head,
and then he SAT so i could put on his leash.

but before we started down the invisible steps,
the big did something unusual.
he spun in a circle, chasing his tail.
"feeling pretty good this morning, are we mr big?"

big didn't answer,
he just took his position at the top of the steps,
and waited on me to descend to the landing,
and tell him to join me.
this was a good routine we developed,
because this process would be a lot riskier on dark mornings,
if the big was on the steps at the same time as me.

we repeated the process on the last steps to the ground,
and after big joined me, i felt his leash twirl again.
"is there a fly after your butt, mr big?"
there was a reason i recognized the twirl of the least when big "chased his tail."
he hates biting flies attacking his butt.
it seemed an oddity.
we don't usually have to worry about the flies until the sun comes up.

about every 10 steps i had to stop again,
and wait while the leash twirled,
and big's feet crunched in the gravel,
as he chased his tail again.
i couldn't imagine what was his issue.
but something was troubling big's tail.

at long last we reached the bottom of the hill,
and came into the circle of illumination underneath the yard light
at the little house.
big took another turn of spinning in circles,
vainly trying to reach his tail.
and under his tail i could see a dark shadow of some sort of
streamer. i reached down and pulled off the dried remains of a
long weed. somehow it had become stuck in the hair on the
bottom of his tail.
problem solved, big was ready to start the serious business of
our morning patrol.

a dog's tail must be a lifelong mystery.
always there,
and always just out of reach.

as our walk progressed, the day's light slowly joined us.
soon i was able to tell why this particular morning had begun
with the pitchest black.
it wasn't just the new moon,
or the thick canopy of the trees overhead.
thick, dark clouds obscured the sky from horizon to horizon.

the morning colors took new tones in the unusual light.
a field of golden wheat, preparing itself to be harvested,
seemed to be the colour of honey.
big himself, appeared to be a dark red.
the trees and pastures were the richest hues of green,
and the reds, blues, purples, yellows and whites of the
wildflowers stood out like lighthouse beacons among the dark
colours of this uniqure morning.
nature never wearies of preparing a new show for us every day.
and me and big never tire of drinking it in.
this morning we walked thru a somber painting of a fantasy
world from a science fiction novel.

we heard the raspy "SKREEE" of the male hawk,
altho we could not locate him.
we made note that none of the hundreds of buzzards that roost
in our valley were visible.
a sure sign that these were not just passing clouds of high fog.
a serious storm was on its way.

we walked past a couple of fields that had been prepared for
planting weeks ago.
but then the work had been postponed as rain after rain
inundated them, turning the ground into impassable mud,
and leaving vast pools of water standing on the rich earth.
farmers always operate at the capricious whims of the weather.
in this case, the luck was not entirely bad.
had the seeds been planted a day earlier,
an entire crop would have drowned.
now the seeds had finally been sown,
and big and i were interested to see one field was filled with
ranks of tiny cornstalks
and the other with the lobe-leafs of soybean seedlings.
like an unfolding mystery,
we would watch the crops and the weather all summer,
to see if this year would bring success or failure to the farmers.

when we at last turned into the driveway,
the rumble of thunder was growing very near,
and the day was growing ominously darker as the thick clouds
turned black and angry.
coming into the woods, i noticed a tall weed growing next to the
driveway.
sandra seems to have a particular objection to having tall weeds
brush her car as she comes and goes, so i absentmindedly took a
swipe at it with my dog trainer to chop it down.
i did not think about how close it was beside me,
nor that i was holding the trainer in the middle,
for balance and ease of carrying.
the result was my back becoming a beta-site for testing the
power of my weapon.

as the top end of the trainer cut down the weedstalk,
the bottom end swung up and smacked into my back, just below
my shoulder blade.

it felt like someone had stuck a branding iron into the flesh of my
back. the intensity of the burning sensation was a total surprise.
and it did not burn for only a moment.
my back was still stinging when we reached the house.

and that was just a short, chopping stroke,
from half the length of the trainer,
with my arm not even extended.
mentally imagining the difference,
with a full arm extension, and getting my back, hips, and legs into
the swing...

no wonder it had turned away the biggest, fiercest dogs;
sending them yelping home.
it must have felt like their skin had been taken off.
that thin, flexible, fiberglass whip packs more pain than being hit
with a baseball bat.
my confidence in the efficacy of this weapon has gone way up.

this morning, when the big white dog made as if he was going to
seriously attack us, i brandished the trainer with confidence,
and told him;
"you better think twice. you get too close and you will feel pain
like you have never felt before."
he hesitated.
dogs can read human body language like a book.
and this book read like a horror story.
"taste this once...."
and i sliced the air with an ominous "WHOOOOOP"
"and you will never want more."
the dog seemed convinced.
at least he backed off.

when we passed him on the way home,
he never budged from his spot in the yard.
i should have done some human trials a long time ago.
but it would have been smarter to swat someone else, and let
them describe it to me.

laz

06-10-13
baby food a-la-diabla (part 1)

lucky for us,
babies don't remember being babies after they grow up.
otherwise, they would come back and kill us for feeding them baby food. eating baby food was hardly the biggest issue of the weekend, but it was easily the most shocking.
how do babies eat that stuff?

but talking about the baby food incident is getting way ahead of myself.

i think i only missed the first running of the kentucky durby.
since then, i have made it an annual pilgrimage,
logging my very mediocre totals year after year.
you see, the durb keeps a record of the all-time results of the durby.
even a plodder like me can eventually begin to pass people.

then stu started coming up and riding with me every year.
the next thing you know, sandra started coming to drive us home. this year case and amy were planning to come and run. lately the durby has been turning into a regular family re-union. this year's reunion would be a memorable one.

as the date of the race approached,
i started having problems with a tooth.
and it wasn't just any tooth.
this tooth was rooted in a tumor that fills about a quarter of my skull. a tumor that does not respond to novocaine.
having had painful dental work done in that area in the past,
i went to great trouble to get a referral to an oral surgeon who does general anaesthesia.
i was pretty unhappy that the best i could do was an appointment the day before the durby.
but we make do with what we have.
dental work was not going to help my performance one bit.
i anticipated an even more mediocre result than usual.
but it wasn't like i had a better choice.

the situation with that tooth was deteriorating rapidly.
it would be a relief to have it gone before the race.

as it turned out, i was not on the same page as the dentist.
his master plan was to stage a $73 appointment,
during which he could glance at the tooth and opine;
"yes, indeed. you, and the other dentist, are both right. that tooth does need to come out."
then i could make yet another appointment to actually do something about it.
i did not relish running the durby with that sore tooth.
but this was the year i would start getting my mileage up to where it took a while for someone to be ahead of me.
besides. once i start on something, i am inclined to see it thru.

later that day,
just as i was fixing to start cooking a chicken for supper,
stu called.
he wanted to go out and eat mexican food.
(who was i to argue with that?)

 about suppertime stu called again.
traffic, traffic, traffic.
he was still hours away,
and i was wishing i had cooked that chicken.
by the time stu got here,
and we drove to his favorite mexican restaurant, it was going to be late.
and i was already starving.

it was sandra who came up with the perfect solution.
this is tennessee, where there are at least two mexican restaurants in every small town.
we could just pick a town halfway to where stu was,
look up a restaurant on the internet,
and meet him there.
brilliant.

i was the only one who didn't have to search for just the right meal. only once have i failed to find my favorite on the menu in a mexican place;
"camerones a la diablo"
no two restaurants prepare it the same,

the big year: winter and spring

but they have all been good.
plus, it should be relatively soft for my painful tooth.
i tried to reccomend it to stu;
explaining that;
"camerones means shrimp. and a la diablo means slightly sweet."

stu is a naturally suspicious person, and chose a different meal.

race morning dawned with great promise.
things had not been going quite according to plan,
but we had surmounted our obstacles.
it was going to be smooth sailing from here on out.

me and big had to start with our usual workout.
coach big does not believe in days off,
even if you are racing later that same day.

as me and big were coming up the drive,
i felt a twinge from that bad tooth.
an ominous twinge.
i commented to stu, as i came inside, that i hoped that tooth
wasn't getting infected.
stu told me i had better not fool around with a possible infection.
i just laughed.
i knew the drill all too well.
if an infection had gotten started in that tumor,
the clock was running.
i would be incapacitated in less than an hour.

an hour later i was rolling in the floor, weeping.
excrutiating pain emanated from my whole head,
and i could not see because of the flashing lights exploding in my
field of vision.

my regular dentist had called in a prescription for antibiotics,
the important thing being to knock down the infection before it
killed me.
he was willing to do that much, but there wasn't going to be a
saturday visit.
i really regretted living in this day and age.
pain killers cannot be called in.
i wasn't sure how long it would take antibiotics to reduce the
infection enough to affect the pain.

i didn't envision that being a quick process.
i was obviously going to have great difficulty at the race.

then amy came in with good news.
her dentist was willing to meet me at his office.
and his office was in nashville, on the way to the race...

we just had to leave a little early.

at what point does a reasonable person just write off a race?
heck, who knows? "reasonable person" doesn't have any application to me anyway.

my vision of just getting something for pain,
so i could see to run,
died on the dentist's chair.
the dentist was determined, that tooth needed to come out NOW.
i tried to explain,
fibroid tumor. novocaine will not go thru it.
he said there were new, and more powerful locals. he could do it.
the tumor is vascularized. it will bleed.
it is hyperennervated. it will hurt.
he was filled with confidence.

we were getting later and later.
i didn't want to miss the start.
like a fool, i agreed.

the first needle went into the roof of my mouth.
there is no way to describe it.
in normal tissue, the needle squirts novocaine ahead,
numbing the tissue before the needle penetrates.
it doesn't work that way in a fibroid.
the needle has to go thru tissue with perfect sensation.
the numbness spreads behind.
i could feel the needle being slowly jammed up thru the roof of my mouth.
i could feel the pressure, as it took a lot of force to drive the needle in.
the dense fibrous tissue of the tumor made a sort of "crunching" sound as the needle went thru.
the pain of the abcessed tooth paled to insignificance.

the big year: winter and spring

i thought i was screaming. but everyone told me i was only moaning.
i know i was concentrating on holding still.
i had learned from countless painful procedures as a child.
no matter how bad the pain, if you don't co-operate it could get worse.

it seemed like it would never end.
the needle kept going further and further,
until i wondered if it would come out inside my nose.
i could swear i finally felt it make contact with the root of my bad tooth.

when he finally got the needle to a point that struck him as deep enough, and pulled it out, the pain did not end.
but at least i could safely writhe in agony and put my hands over my face.
he kept telling me; "give it 5 minutes, give it 5 minutes."
i give dr m a lot of credit,
he has a good game face. he barely showed that he had not really expected what happened.
his assistant looked more concerned.
when the pain finally subsided,
and i was lying there breathing hard
(real pain is a huge physical strain)
he asked me if i wanted to continue.
there was only one real choice.
"no. i don't want to continue. i would rather die.
but if we don't finish, then i have to start this all over again on another day....

i am assuming you aren't willing to kill me instead?"

the next needle came from the outside, and went thru my gums.
that is not pleasant, but,
if you ever have to make that choice,
a needle thru the gums is a thousand times easier than one thru the palate.
when he finally finished, the assistant asked him if he needed another needle.
"there is no way he can feel anything thru that much anaesthetic."

then he tapped the end of the bad tooth.
it was like a jolt of electricity.
"i told you there was a reason i did not want to be awake for this."

i don't know how many needles it took.
he would locate un-numbed tissue with the needle, and hit it,
then move on.
i started to feel wierd from all the local in my head.
finally, the dr said;
"i cannot put any more than this in one patient."
but it was about as good as it was going to get.
i could barely feel any part of my mouth anymore.

the actual surgery part wasn't so bad.
after the tooth came out, i couldn't feel the rest of his work at all.
 (as my tongue discovered later) he cut down deep
and put in a bone graft.
there was lots of pushing and working to get things like he wanted.
counting the stitches as he finished up,
i knew he had done a good bit of cutting.
i was pretty determined not to leave without some serious pain pills. the numbness would not last forever.

sandra, on the other hand, kept asking;
"all he needs is tylenol, right?"
sandra's basic approach to medical care is;
"you will either live, or you will die. just don't spend any money."
thank god he gave me a prescription after she left.

then he started with the instructions;
"don't go anywhere for a couple of days..."
"we're on our way to a race!"

i left under the agreement i wasn't going to take part. just watch.
that seemed reasonable enough.
after my morning, i didn't feel a whole lot like running any more.
we checked the time. at least we still had time to get there....

to be continued.

laz

06-10-13
baby food a-la-diabla (part 2)

case and lex, with the burrito,
had to come by the dentist office to get their camping stuff.
sandra left with them for the race,
so stu and me were bringing up the rear.
that was our lucky break for the day,
because we were barely out of nashville before the phone rang...

sandra's party was about 60 miles ahead of us;
sitting in a traffic jam 15 miles short of the kentucky line.

forewarned, we used a parallel highway to bypass the tie-up.
cleverly we re-entered the interstate just a couple of miles past the problem.
but before we could congratulate ourselves, we ran smack into another traffic jam,
just across the state line.
this time there was no alternative route to take.

it took a while, moving a few car lengths at a time,
before we finally discovered the source of the stoppage.
it was a failure of traffic control.
we eventually came to a sign which said;
"lane closure ahead"
much later we came to a sign which said;
"merge left"
now, if everyone were to merge left at that point,
traffic would have barely slowed,
all the cars would have narrowed to one lane,
and buzzed right through the construction zone...

people will not do that without police cars ahead,
slapping enormous, painful tickets on those who cannot work with others.
so, instead, all the vehicles driven by selfish jerks continue in the closed lane,
right up to the closure,
where they try to jam in, ahead of everyone who can work co-operatively with others.

as a result, everyone comes to a stop...
including the jerks.
their selfishness, fittingly, costs them time as well as everyone else.
there should be a lesson in this.

stu and i entertained ourselves by thinking of appropriate punishments.
fortunately, we had left with about 9 hours to make a 3 hour drive.
much of the cushion had been eaten up,
what with emergency surgeries and all,
but we still had time to spare.

obviously the easy answer was for the state highway patrol to do their job.
they could have reaped a bonanza in tickets for a while...
until the traffic recognized the threat and started going thru the construction zones as they should.
these days traffic enforcement prefers the steady cash flow of the hidden cameras.
what with abbreviated yellow lights, speed-trap zones out in the woods on major highways,
and other such tricks,
the revenue can be maintained regardless of how people drive.
and no actual work is involved,
beyond some clerk sending letters to notify people they have been robbed.

we finally got thru that construction zone,
and drove about 50 miles before hitting another.
this time we came up with better plans than mere tickets.
i wanted to pull the miscreants out of their cars,
when they reached the convergence in the wrong lane,
kill them and leave the bodies alongside the highway.
stu pointed out we would accomplish nothing by killing only the drivers.
we needed to exterminate the entire family,
and eliminate the tainted bloodlines from the gene pool.

by the next traffic jam,
i was ready to up the ante.

the big year: winter and spring

i wanted to stick a needle in the roof of these people's mouths.
then kill them.

the burrito party was still ahead of us,
and they called to report one final traffic jam,
inside paducah.

they had plenty of time to call,
as they were stopped on the roadside,
fixing a flat tire.

assuming we ever made it,
the race would hopefully be easier than the "short" drive to get there.

stu and i pulled up as the field was receiving its final instructions,
and stu hurried over to join them.
i set my chair out.
i had compromised on my instructions to go home and rest
with an agreement to sit in my chair and watch the race.

since no one seemed to be monitoring me
(and pumped full of pain pills)
i sort of meandered to the back of the pack.
what could it possibly hurt to walk one slow lap?

i was so slow that everyone lapped me at least twice.
and by the time i reached the end of the lap,
the whole field was lined up again for the "restart."
the new electronic timing system had passed all the dry runs
only to fail once the real event was under way.

i sat down and regrouped while the field took off again.
then i discretely moseyed back onto the track.
i was going to get at least one lap after everything i had gone thru
to get here.

by the time i reached the end of this even slower lap,
the race had stopped while the old timing system was reinstalled
for the second restart.

at this point, i was becoming painfully aware that i had not eaten
in 36 hours...
save for a bowl of vegetable soup with no vegetables

(i think that is called flavored water)
sandra took me to the store to find something to eat.

i returned to the track with a selection of baby food.
i picked out one euphemistically called "turkey and rice"
i like turkey and rice.
i like a lot of things.
actually there are only 3 things i cannot stand in any form;
cucumbers, peanut butter....

and sweet potatoes.
case would later read the fine print on the second, unused,
package of "turkey and rice"
those bums had snuck in (for reasons no-one can fathom) sweet
potatoes.
i renamed the stuff "would taste better after passing thru a baby"
i was hungry enough to eat the back end out of a rag doll.
the back end out of a rag doll would have been better.
unfortunately, it would have meshed poorly with my mouthful of
stitches.
after forcing down the nasty mess, i had no further desire to eat.
i gave the remaining baby food to case and lex, for the burrito.
i can only hope she forgets this when she grows up.
or she will come back and kill me.

i took another pain pill, and watched the runners circle for a few
minutes.
then i quietly slipped back on the track.
i was going to log a lap in this race.
no matter how many times i had to do it.

to be continued

laz

06-10-13
baby food a-la-diabla (part 3)

as i trudged around the track on my groundhog lap 3,
i had determined that neither of the c's was there this year.
asking around, i found out s had hurt her ankle playing
volleyball.
this was particularly frustrating news.
i had beaten s by the narrowest margin the first time we raced,
in the death match on the river.
in subsequent deathmatches, she had hammered me pretty good.

but getting hammered pretty good only builds a deficit of so
many miles.
it wasn't like i had not logged miles of my own.
while she was at home, propping a sore ankle,
i could have made up a lot of ground.
considering how good my conditioning when i left home,
i might have even caught her.

while i was pondering this,
i was nearing the end of my third first lap.
since it was obvious i could do more than one lap,
i decided that a whole mile was a lot more desireable than a half
mile.
so i continued right on past my chair.

during that lap i started to feel sort of funny.
all that novocaine, or whatever local he used,
left my head all tingly.
and my stomach something less than tingly.
or maybe it was the growing span of time without food
(baby food not counting as actual food)
or maybe that is just what happens after oral surgery.
at any rate, it seemed like a good idea to sit and watch the race...

like i had promised.

while i sat, i saw that it was in the second hour,
and i had two laps.
a lap an hour seemed like a good compromise.
A lap an hour was pretty much the same as just watching.

i would still be mostly watching.
my mouth hadn't started bleeding.
and sitting there i started to feel a lot better.

so when the 3rd hour began,
i started another lap.
while i was doing that lap,
it struck me that i might not be able to do a lap every hour.
maybe i'd be better off to get my 10 laps as expediently as possible.

even moving at a sluggish 15 minutes per lap
my mouth was starting to grow painful.
it was a lucky thing i thought to string some laps together.
with 15 minutes left in the third hour
i retreated to my chair and took another pain pill.
with 5 laps down, i could afford to recuperate until the halfway mark of the race.

at the start of the 4th hour, i returned to the track.
i am just not very good at resting.
my mouth didn't hurt any more,
but i was a little woozy from the pain medicine.
so i settled back into a very slow 15 minutes per lap.

after that i just kept moving.
i like to keep moving.
10 laps came and went.

when my mouth started hurting,
i checked to be sure it wasn't bleeding, took another pain pill,
and kept moving.
the pain pills would never make the cut as a performance enhancer.
i found myself weaving between the lanes of the track.
i just stayed outside so i wouldn't interfere with the people who were actually running.

once in a while someone would stop and talk.
god only knows what i told them.
sandra had been totally enthralled with the burrito,
And spent the whole time playing with the baby.
so there was no one to tell me to stop.

i spent a lot of time thinking of foods that were soft enough to eat (except baby food)
almost before i knew it, light was spreading over the track.
i completed my 33rd lap without time to do another and went to sit down.
16-1/2 miles was no where near what i had wanted.
but it sure beat nothing.
then i found out i would get credit for the false start laps.
17.5
i wondered if that was good enough to move me up on the all-time list.
i wondered how close it put me to savannah.
i wondered where was the closest place to buy some runny eggs.
i was sure enough hungry.

big would be waiting for me when i got home,
and tomorrow would start my final push to get ready for the met-a-mosquito 100km.

i sure hope the trip to that race goes better than this one did.

laz

06-14-13
the big winner

big was sitting in the shade when amy drove by.
i was out in the sun, pushing the mower.
amy stopped, and i told her;
"just look at big. he is right where i told him to STAY."
amy laughed.
"so he won. he got exactly what he wanted."
i looked at big.
his eyes were half shut.
his mouth open in that impossibly wide grin.
"no... not exactly."

the big is a very obedient dog.
he likes to be told what to do,
and he likes to do it.
but he has this one issue...

he wants to be with me all the time.
i understand now, why so many pit rescues won't give out a dog,
unless it gets to live in the house.
big likes dogs, even tho he is bit socially awkward.
he adores his family.
and lives for his master.

the first of big's "wins" was his move to the porch.
first during rainstorms.
then during the night.
these days big is only on his cable when we have company.
he stays on the porch like he has been told.
he only goes off to use the bathroom,
check my car for squirrels,
or greet visitors...

unexpected visitors, or old friends.
otherwise he is on his cable.
we don't (usually) tell them he can take the cable off if he feels
like it.

on the back porch, big contentment has increased exponentially.
with all the windows to look in,
he seems to feel that he is now a part of the household.
it was sort of uncomfortable at first.
we'd all be in the common room,
talking, laughing, doing whatever,
and i would look at the door,
and there was big.
looking in with his silly grin, wagging his tail.
as far as big is concerned,
he is not the least shut out, or treated poorly.
he is part of the family.
it is all he ever wanted.

well, that and accompanying his master everywhere.

the only way i can leave the house without putting the big guy on his cable
is to sneak out the garage and get in amy or sandra's car.
he isn't that concerned with their comings and goings.
if i open my own car door...

the big year: winter and spring

big is there when i get inside;
looking at me hopefully and wagging his tail.
if i start to walk somewhere;
big is there in a flash.
following me.

where i had real issues was mowing the yard at the little house at the bottom of the hill.
super ears can hear me perfectly.
and no matter how i emphasize he STAY on his cable,
he can only stand it so long before he has to come and join me.
mowing was taking twice as long,
altho i was getting in lots of extra miles taking big back and returning him to his cable.

sometimes i didn't even get back to the mower.
i would hear big stop barking
(to warn me he had accidentally been left on his cable)
and just turn to wait.
in about 15 seconds i would see him come around the corner heading down the driveway.
he stopped as soon as he saw me,
and waited while i came back up.
when i passed him he would fall in behind me...

walking slowly with his head hanging.

once or twice i caught him peeking at me from behind trees in the woods.
the old boy was nothing if he wasn't determined.

a wise dog trainer once told me to set my dogs up to succeed.
it was pretty obvious that this approach wasn't setting big up to succeed.
i needed a new approach.
something big could do.

i took him with me a couple of times to mow the septic area down back.
it is a small clearing in the middle of the woods,
a perfect place to do some training.

at first, every time i stopped, big's nose hit the back of my leg.
he followed me around and around while i pushed the mower,
about a foot behind me.
it didn't matter how hot the sun was.
(now i know what they mean by "dogging" someone's footsteps)
pretty soon he figured out i was going nowhere.
then it was easy to get him to understand that his job was to lie
in the shade and watch me.
at first i had to stay in sight, or he would move.
later he was ok as long as he could hear me.
he would STAY where i put him.

the real test would be at the little house,
where there would be cars and people and other dogs,
not just squirrels and rabbits and turkey.
the real test was today.

my first thought was that maybe all that work on STAY would
give me another option. i went out thru the garage, grabbed the
gas can and started down the driveway.
big materialized behind me.
i turned and told him;
"you have to wait on the porch big guy. go STAY on the porch."
big turned and started for the porch, head hanging.
i started back down the hill, and after a short distance stopped
and looked back.

big had followed a few steps.
"BIG. you have to STAY on the porch big. STAY."
big just looked at me.
i went a little further and looked again.
big was gone.
i checked in the woods.
no big peeking around a tree.
(i know dogs are not that clever. but this was the big.)

i checked again before i went around the first curve out of sight.
no big.

i checked a couple more times.
i was almost at the bottom of the hill, and feeling cocky, when
amy came driving up,
heading for the house.

the big year: winter and spring

"i got big to STAY on the porch!"
amy laughed.
"no you didn't."

i looked back up the drive,
and there was big.
he had come around a curve about 50 yards back and was
standing, looking at us.
i couldn't see the expression on his face, but i didn't need to.
it was the expression that says i am about to take him to the
house and put him on his cable.

amy went on, leaving me and the big looking at each other.
"well, big guy. you might as well come on."
big took off running to join me.
this time his expression said;
"i am the happiest dog on earth!"

we went to the little house.
in the morning there is shade on one side.
in the afternoon the shade is on the other.
i put him in the morning shade and told him to STAY.
i had to put him back one time,
then he STAYED.
i went in the little house and got him a bowl of water.
i set it on one of the flat rocks that punctuate our lawn,
just to emphasize that this was his place.

i divided the yard into small sections,
and started out mowing the ones where i was close and he could
see me the whole time.
then i moved on to places where i was temporarily out of sight,
and finally the other end of the house,
where he could only see me briefly on each round.
all he did was move down a little, so he could see me better.

when i finished a tank of gas,
i got a drink of gatorade,
and went to tell big what a good, smart dog he was.
he fairly beamed with pride.
big loves to be told what to do.
and he loves doing it.
he flopped over on his back to beg for a belly runb,

and i gave him a good belly rub.
then he thrashed around in the grass on his back, laughing.
most dogs laugh with a breathy "ha-ha-ha" sound.
big, with his short nose, has a sort of a grunt in his laugh.
it sounds frighteningly human.
big doesn't laugh that much,
but he felt exceptionally good about this morning.

he passed all the tests.
cars passed.
people passed.
mr winston's new dog came down the road and stopped to bark at me...

until she spotted big lying in the grass with no leash,
then she took off for home.

big never left his spot.

afternoon came,
and i moved big across the yard to a new shade spot
(his old shade being nearly gone)
and i mowed the side of the yard where he had been in the morning.
big performed like a champ.

he was still lying there in the shade when amy left for work.
i was out in the sun, pushing the mower.
amy stopped, and i told her;
"just look at big. he is right where i told him to STAY."
amy laughed.
"so he won. he got exactly what he wanted."
i looked at big.
his eyes were half shut.
his mouth open in that impossibly wide grin.
"no... not exactly."

i mean, it wasn't really like big won.
i just changed my tactics....

right?

laz

About the Author

Lazarus Lake did not write this book; he merely recorded the stories that Big shared with him. They live on a small farm in Tennessee where they train and organize popular ultra-marathons, a world-wide community that Laz has been a part of for over 3 decades and Big first joined a couple of years ago.

Made in the USA
Lexington, KY
10 March 2015